Improve Relationship EQ

by Improving Your Attachment Style

Isabel B. Kirk
MA, LPC

"No more questions, no more unknowns, this is it. It's the feeling of bond-ness with other people, not with just one person, but with many people – some of whom may be friends, intimate friends, lovers, mates, children, but people. It feels like you belong to people from whom you get your needs met. Bottom line- that's what it's all about. Not the pain, not the fortune, not the success, not the struggle, just the love. It's a beautiful feeling. I wish you could all feel it."

Daniel Casriel, MD

Table Of Contents

Chapter One 10
  Introduction To Attachment Theory
    What Is A Relationship And Why Do They Matter?
    How Attachment Plays A Role In Relationships
      History Of Attachment Theory
      The Parent-Child Bond
    Love And Attachment: A Theory Emerges
      What Is Love?
      Love As A Survival Need

Chapter Two 23
  My Attachment Style
    An Introduction To Attachment Styles And How They Develop
    Attachment Starts In Infancy
    The Roots Of Impaired Attachment
    Determining My Own Attachment Style!
    The Different Styles Of Attachment
    Attachment Styles In Relationships

Chapter Three 54
  Deepening "Whole" Self Awareness Through Eight Parts
    Part One: Awareness Of My Current Thoughts, Feelings And Behaviors
    Part Two: Awareness Of My Early Attachment Experiences
    Part Three: Awareness Of My Imago

Part Four: Awareness Of My True Needs

Part Five: Awareness Of My Underlying Childhood Assumptions

Part Six: Awareness Of The Roots Of My Frustrations

Part Seven: Awareness Of How I Feel Most Taken Care Of

Part Eight: Awareness Of Hidden Agendas And Expectations

Chapter Four 116

Healthy Attachment And Retraining Your Brain

Step One: Embracing My Feelings

- Validating And Soothing Our Feelings
- Mindful Observance
- Inner Child Work

Step Two: Connecting With My Cognitive Thinking Patterns

- Identifying My Beliefs
- Connecting My Beliefs With My Feelings

Step Three: Taking Action Towards Change

Step Four: Cultivating A Secure Attachment

- What Secure Attachment Looks Like
- Secure Communication Skills
- Final Suggestions And Tools

Copyright and Disclaimer

© Copy right 2015 by Isabel B. Kirk, LPC. All rights reserved. No part of this book may be reproduced or transmitted in any form, by any means, (electronic, photocopying, recording or otherwise) without the prior written permission of the author. No liability is assumed with respect to the use of the information contained within. Although every precaution has been taken, the author assumes no liability for errors or omissions. Neither is any liability assumed for damages resulting for the use of the information contained herein.

IMPORTANT NOTE: The approach in this book assumes that if in a relationship, it is a generally healthy one. If you are in an unhealthy or abusive relationship, it is strongly recommended that you seek professional mental health services.

This book in intended for information and educational purposes only. It is not a substitute for consultation with a mental health professional and should not be construed as a form of, or substitute for counseling, psychotherapy, or other psychological service.

Edited by Carla Dippel

Cover Designed by Sharon Julien

Preface And Acknowledgements

When I decided to become a therapist, I did it as part of my own journey in search of happiness and fulfillment. As I worked my way through many years of studies, every expert and study concludes that the ultimate source of happiness is in relationships. Since then, I became intrigued and passionate about them; this is how I came upon the theory of attachment.

I realized that there was a way to identify the problem and its origins, but that it was a whole different story to solve it. This led me to further investigation and experts who have dedicated their lives and talents to the development of treatment modalities which can help us repair the wounding that relationship problems cause in the first place and show us what a healthy relationship looks like and how to achieve it. Now that we finally have a more scientific understanding of what love is and how to have it in our lives as a source of happiness and health, as it should be, I feel a strong desire to share this information so everybody can enjoy it.

I want to profoundly thank all the experts in the attachment field and relationship theorists who I have learned from immensely. I would like to especially thank professors Cindy Hazan and Phillip Shaver, R. Chris Fraley from the University of Illinois, Dr. Amir Levine and Rachel Heller, Dr. Susan Johnson and Dr. Harville Hendrix, Dianne

Poole, PhD, Laurel Parnell, PhD, and Shirley Jean Schmidt, LPC as well as pioneers John Bolwby and Mary Ainsworth.

Last but not least, I would like to thank professors Daniel Siegel and Allan Shore. Siegel is considered the father of interpersonal neurobiology for his approach of developing a healthy mind, an integrated brain, and empathic relationships. Shore's groundbreaking integration of neuroscience with attachment theory has led to his description as "the American Bowlby."

And especially and most sincerely, I am thankful to the people who allow me into their lives day to day and teach me the most valuable lessons of life, humanity and love: my clients.

About The Author

Isabel B. Kirk is a Bilingual Licensed Professional Counselor Psychologist serving the Northern Virginia and Washington, DC metropolitan areas. With more ten years in the counseling field, Isabel draws from her own personal journey, professional intuition and extensive training to help people improve their lives. She works with individuals, couples, families and groups from different backgrounds and situations, helping them to not only solve problems but to also have more fulfilling and connected lives. She lives with her husband and her two children in Annandale, VA.

Find out more about at www.dcvacounseling-psychotherapy.com

Isabel B. Kirk, MA, LPC

Licensed Professional Counselor

Attachment Relationships Therapist

Eating Disorder Specialist & Intuitive Eating Counselor

EMDR & Internal Family Systems Practitioner

Introduction

You might be thinking "oh... another self-help book." Understandable. I have read them all, and contrary to popular belief, a book is not going to fix our problems. But this is not just another self-help book. The purpose of this guide is to describe the basic but fundamental aspects that take place in relationship dynamics. Why is this not just another self-help book? There are plenty out there and they do a good job of covering whatever their subject matter is. They are usually written by well-known experts in the field and based on years of scientific research. However, there are not many resources that lay out a clear, deep and realistic pathway of the personal journey and intrinsic work that improving your relationships involves. People spend precious time and energy on multiple books and resources to gain some idea of what applies to them. Sometimes they get so overwhelmed with the search, they stop trying altogether. Here I have summarized the most useful information and knowledge I have received from training, text books, self-help books, and clinical and personal experience in order to explain in simple terms what everybody needs to know about the basics of relationship dynamics and what roles we play in them.

It is important to understand our role in relationships so that we aren't victims of our past. By understanding our unconscious we can set ourselves free. We can't change what we don't know. Once we identify our role in a relationship, we can take care of the aspects that we can change and accept the ones we cannot. Also, by understanding the basics of relationships dynamics, we won't go on blindly repeating past experiences over and over again or putting all the responsibility on ourselves or the other person to make the relationship better. By knowing what we offer and receive in relationships and acting upon that knowledge, we can learn how to change our patterns and ultimately avoid the pain and disappointment that unhealthy relationships bring.

Relationships are the key to human happiness. People with strong and broad social relationships are happier, healthier and live longer. Close relationships with family and friends provide love, meaning, and support and increase our feelings of self worth. Scholars and scientists agree on the central importance of relationships for our wellbeing and happiness. Dr. John Medina, a developmental molecular biologist and dad, in his book *Brain Rules for the Baby*, emphasizes that at the end of the day people who are the happiest and most successful are the ones that have healthy relationships. He says to not worry about raising your children to be rich or smart, but happy. The way to do that is to have a good relationship with them. Dr. Sue Johnson (a bestselling author, clinical psychologist, and recognized innovator who has changed the field of couples therapy based on her discoveries about attachment) also reassures us that "A good relationship is the best recipe for happiness and good health and a powerful antidote to aging." (Johnson, Love Sense, 2013)

Taking action to strengthen our relationships and build connections is essential for happiness. The problem is that people keep trying through their own strategies, which only leads to more pain and frustration. Or they give up, depriving themselves of one of the most wonderful human experiences. Even though this guide will focus mostly on romantic intimate relationships, you will soon realize that you can apply the same principles to all your relationships.

> "For one human being to love another: that is perhaps the most difficult of all our tasks, the ultimate, the last test and proof, the work for which all other work is but preparation."
>
> Rainer Maria Rilke

Another purpose of this guidebook is to be the bridge between polarized views of "normalcy" and trauma in literature. Many people, including my clients, report that the majority of books mention cases of severe child abuse or extreme clinical family dysfunction. This displeases them because they feel it is not similar to their own case, and it also makes them feel guilty (apparently their life was pretty good compared to the people in the cases described). Finding help though this kind of literature can be counterproductive because people end up feeling that they should not have any problems. This leads to further invalidation of their personal truths and feeling "unworthy" of help. Though it is undeniable that extreme situations do cause trauma, less obvious deficiencies or "ordinary trauma" can be as equally damaging as abuse, leaving individuals unable to maintain healthy relationships. In this guide I will make reference to cases and people like you and me who are common, healthy and functional but who have some struggles dealing with relationships due to what I call "cracks" in the foundation. Many times subtle day to day deficiencies or interactions cause "ordinary trauma" which prevents people from making or maintaining healthy relationships. Ordinary trauma happens in the best and most caring families because it is usually caused by subtle deficiencies or life circumstances more than by obvious abuse or neglect. You will learn more about this in the following pages.

In this guide I will address relationship dynamics and how you can improve them by introducing you to something called *attachment theory*. This is the latest theory that explains human relationships and the nature of how we bond. Throughout this guide you will learn what attachment is and how you can earn a secure one.

I want to emphasize that attachment happens on a continuum; the results from this guidebook will depend on where you fall on it. Some people may gain a lot from reading and doing the exercises in this guide and move significantly towards a secure attachment. Others may gain more insight and validation about their situation and feel satisfied with that; at least they will understand why things don't work or why they feel the way they feel, and that in itself is plenty. Others will realize they need deeper work and that connecting with a therapist, especially in the beginning, is what is needed. This is another reason why this is not just another self-help book. Not everybody will earn a secure attachment by only reading and following this book (like most self-help literature promises). Attachment is a much more complicated matter and is a relational process, so cultivation of healthy attachment in a relationship setting will make the most sense. "Before there is a Self, there is a relationship...and it is from that relationship that the self emerges"- L. Alan Sroufe

I really want to emphasize this point. Many times we read a book and we end up feeling more frustrated because we cannot follow the wonderful advice and clear steps pointed out in it. It is not that simple. People who can simply do the steps (turn their mind to positive thoughts, follow a diet and lose a few pounds, bounce back sooner from break ups and disappointments, follow simple action steps to improve their relationships) are people who are probably closer to a secure attachment to begin with. For the majority of us, we "get it" but we can't apply it. Why? Because at the crucial moment when your insecure attachment is activated, it doesn't matter how much good, logical information you have learned; you feel you just can't follow those steps, and then you feel remorse for it. Most people will need the nurturing of a relationship to get some healing and to start to flourish.

This is why I am calling this a guidebook. My hope is to provide clarity about what is going on, why you feel the way you feel and do what you do, why it is ok if you want a healthy relationship, why it is not just your partner who is wrong, etc. It will guide your way towards earning that secure attachment which will then help you implement all the wonderful research-founded information out there about how to better your relationships. This guidebook is a tool that you can use within a close relationship or safe therapeutic environment. It will provide you with two important elements for healing: 1) intrapsychic work or internal attachment (individual personal healing mostly through awareness and meditation) and 2) relational work or relational attachment (external healing mostly through working with partners and in therapy). For some people who have attachment wounds, their family and partner relationships may not be healthy enough to provide the elements for gaining a secure attachment. For this group of people, the therapeutic relationship is usually the only safe and secure environment to experience what secure attachment looks and feels like for the first time. Some recommendations on how to go about this approach are at the end of this book.

Whether you follow this guide completely and practice the exercises and recommendations from cover to cover, do some of them or just read it, my most sincere hope is that you gain awareness into your relational world and improve your relationship EQ, gaining a new lens through which to explore your daily interactions and relational choices. The change or healing that is possible may be a longer process than you are ready to embark on right now. Regardless of the stage you are in, you will be able to look at and perceive your relationships (intimate romantic ones, friends, coworkers and neighbors) differently. Hopefully this will open the door to more understanding and compassion, allowing you to embrace and accept the quirks as well as the potential of social human nature.

As much as the purpose of this guidebook is to encourage change, it is equally important to emphasize that for some the majority of healing will be in embracing the process and not the outcome. In other words, you may find some peace by simply understanding and accepting your imperfect nature. Instead of looking for the right person in the typical way of "how I want you to be" and "you should be," we can be gentler with relationship expectations by understanding our attachment habits. We can take our relationship as a life-long journey where, through daily challenges, enlightenment and love, we can not only pull through but become stronger. In the end, we don't have to be perfect to be loved (which is what we all desire deep down).

So I invite you to have fun while embarking on this fantastic and courageous journey of self-discovery in the context of your relationships! If you are still wondering what this is all about, let me tell you what the prizes are. In this journey you will gain insight into the following aspects:

1. The innate need to relate, which we all experience as part of being human in order to survive. Relationships are the social being's method of fulfilling physical, psychological, and social development. Healthy relationships produce the nourishment and security needed to live and thrive.

   "The first and foremost instinct of humans is neither sex nor aggression. It is to connect. The need for connection is our first and most primary instinct. Romantic love is an attachment bond, just like that between mother and child."- Susan Johnson, PhD.

2. The reality that even though we believe we actively choose unique partners and relationships, we are still fully influenced by the unconscious.

"Partner selection is the result of an unconscious match between a mental image of one's parents/caretakers, created in childhood (called Imago) and certain character traits of the attractive partner."- Harville Hendrix, PhD.

3. A review of your own relational history and experiences (internal/intrapersonal factors and external/environmental factors).

"Only in a relationship can you know yourself, not in abstraction, and certainly not in isolation."- J. Krishnamurti.

4. Typical mating patterns and how to determine your style.

"From suffering I have learned this: that whoever is wounded by love will never be made whole unless she embraces the very same love which wounded her."- Mechtild of Magdeburg.

5. An understanding of the idea that as adults we no longer have to be victims of our pasts. We can accept and love ourselves and others while working to change what we can change and accept what we cannot.

"At each moment we choose the intentions that will shape our experiences and those things upon which we will focus our attention. If we choose unconsciously, we evolve unconsciously. If we choose consciously, we evolve consciously."- Gary Zukow.

6. If you are a parent you get an extra bonus! Because attachment is a universal need, the attachment view of love can also help parents understand conflicts with their children.

" When we get a better understanding of what love is really about, we can know how to sustain it and better nurture it with our partners and families." - Susan Johnson, PhD.

CHAPTER ONE

Introduction To Attachment Theory

WHAT IS A RELATIONSHIP AND WHY DO THEY MATTER?

The first concept I'd like to emphasize is that the need for relationships is as basic to all human beings as food: it is a survival response (Johnson, Hold Me Tight, 2008). Attachment lives deep in primordial pathways in the brain. We are social creatures; the survival and evolution of the human race has depended on it! Our brains develop in relationships and without them we would die as babies or develop mental illnesses as adults.

Our need to feel connected to other people, to love and be loved, to care and be cared for, is a fundamental human need. Some experts argue that the capacity to love and be loved is the most important human strength. So to begin, I am going to describe what a relationship is.

An interpersonal relationship is a relatively long-term association between two or more people. This association may be based on emotions like love and liking, need, or some other type of social commitment (Webster Dictionary). The main types of relationships are intimate, friends, business, and societal. Other thinkers have described relationships as:

"The strong emotional tie that a person feels toward a special other person in his or her life." (Lefton, 2005)

"A relatively enduring emotional tie to a specific other person." (Maccoby, 1980)

As you can see, all these definitions involve the notion of emotions and another person. This is because relationships are actually the product of our need to emotionally bond to another human being for healthy physical, psychological, and social development. We are social beings; we cannot live in isolation.

HOW ATTACHMENT PLAYS A ROLE IN RELATIONSHIPS

So what is this amazing "attachment" process?

Attachment refers to the particular way in which you relate to other people. Your style of attachment was mostly formed in the very beginning of your life, during your first two years. The adaptations we make to the interactive relationships between ourselves and our early caretakers impact every area of our lives as adults, from how we parent to how we treat our partner. The particular attachment style we develop strongly colors the lens through which we view the world and other people. This lens is referred to as our "working model." We come to see the world as safe and positive, unsafe and dangerous, or a combination of these perspectives. In relationships, our working model of attachment influences how each of us reacts to our needs and how we go about getting them met. We will explore the impact of negative working models versus healthy working models throughout the rest of this book.

According to the revolutionary attachment theory pioneered by English psychiatrist John Bowlby:

> "Attachment is the result of the bonding process that occurs between a child and caregiver during the first couple years of the child's life. This bond is the primary force in infant development." (Bowlby, 1969 & Aisnworth, 1973)

Attachment theory was extended to adult romantic relationships in the late 1980's by Cindy Hazan and Phillip Shaver. Since then, the bonding process is used as a theoretical framework to explain adult relationships. Two main theories in the field expand on this concept: Imago Theory developed by Harville Hendrix, PhD and Emotionally Focused Therapy (EFT) created by Susan Johnson, PhD. We will interact more with these theories in later chapters.

HISTORY OF ATTACHMENT THEORY

The theory of attachment is one of the latest in human development. Psychologists and researchers have dedicated the last fifty years to really understanding a concept that since the 1700's was a mystery for many.

Certain priests in the 1760's were the first to notice children dying in orphanages even though they were being fed and taken care of. The same phenomenon happened more recently with children in Romanian orphanages. This is when the first clues were identified: these children were dying of emotional starvation.

It wasn't until the 1930's and 1940's that psychiatrist and psychologist John Bolwby began to develop a theory that has helped clarify a lot of questions about personal interaction. After World War II, he conducted a research study with children who were left as a result of the war. He found that children who were separated from caretakers during their first years of life had difficulty engaging with other people later in life, and some of them developed what he called an "affectionless" emotional state.

War was not the only circumstance in which children got separated from their parents in early life. A second attempt to prove his theory was in the 1950's when he verified the same symptoms in children who were deprived of parental visits while being in the hospital. As a result of his studies, the policy that allowed parents to visit their child only one hour per week was changed. Other circumstances such as disease, death, and post partum depression were also shown to produce similar symptoms in children later in life.

These findings represented a revolutionary change in the world of psychology. Freud, who is still the father of psychology, had focused his studies on "intra-psychic" factors as the causes of pathology.

Bolwby introduced the concept of external/relational factors as additional causes of pathology.

Freud-Traditional Psychology	Bowlby's - New Psychology
Human deregulations are result of internal predisposition or genes	Human deregulations are a result of interpersonal interactions
Promote independence	Promotes interdependence

Bowlby changed the focus of traditional psychology because he promoted the idea that healthy relationships and interactions were not only the product of our internal factors (nature: genes, hard wired brain structures) but also a product of our relationships and experiences in life (environment: parent-child, friends, teachers, day care, school, physical moves, living situations etc). His studies set the precedent for later discoveries which proved that inter-dependence is an intrinsic need not only for physical survival but for emotional wellbeing and therefore, overall quality of life.

THE PARENT-CHILD BOND

Bowlby and other researchers (Ainsworth, 1978; Hazan & Shaver, 1987) concluded that the parent-child bond provides an irreplaceable context for emotional development, and that an infant's initial bond with primary caregivers affects how that individual will approach relationships in the future. This was a revolutionary concept.

We have come to learn that attachment benefits both the child and the caregiver by:

- Providing and seeking comfort for distress
- Providing and experiencing warmth, empathy and nurturance
- Providing emotional availability and regulating emotions
- Providing and seeking physical and psychological protection

(Zeanah & Smyke, 2008 as cited in Potter & Sullivan)

Caregivers who are generally sensitive, responsive and available have infants with internal representations of themselves as loveable and worthy. Attachment theory opened the door to understanding and making sense of love.

> "Although the nature of love is not easy to define, it has an intrinsic order, a structure that can be detected, excavated, and explored. Emotional experience, in all its resplendent complexity, cannot emerge ex vacuo. It must originate in dynamic neural systems humming with physiological machinations as specific and patterned as they are intricate."
> (Lewis, T., Amini, F., & Lannon, R, Theory of Love, 2001)

Despite these scientific advances, for the major part of the 20th century the study of relationships did not include its physiological aspect. It wasn't until recent decades that the explosion of neuroscience began to focus on explaining how the brain is the only organ that transforms or develops its physical structure by experiences. Since a brain cannot develop in isolation, the experiences that have the most influence on the developing brain are those acquired through intimate relationships. Video-based studies of infants and their caregivers conducted in thousands of homes around the world have illustrated the influence of the attachment bond on the nervous system. Such research has led to the conclusion that the attachment bond relationship plays a dominant role in the development of the brain, the individual, and his or her connection to others and the world. "Experience Grows the Brain. The brain develops by forming connections. Interactions with caregivers are critical to brain development. The more an experience is repeated, the stronger the connections become." (National Child Stress Traumatic Network, 2003)

In his book *"The Developing Mind,"* Daniel J. Siegel, the father of modern interpersonal neurobiology, uses the phrase "the feeling of being felt" to describe relationships that shape the mental circuits responsible for memory, emotion, and self-awareness. Brain-altering communication is triggered by deeply felt emotions which register in facial expressions, eye contact, touch, posture, movements, pace and timing, intensity, and tone of voice. These concepts are huge since they support former premises of a more scientific explanation of what love is and also what a healthy display of it looks like. Most authors consider a healthy relationship to be the achieved balance of independence and dependency between the parts, resulting in inter-dependence. Siegel (2010) also refers to it as the internal concepts of the "Me" and the "We" and the balanced interaction between both.

Bowlby sustained that attachment happened during the first years of life. Now we know that attachment is a life-long process. We don't stop attaching, and attachment can change. A child can attach to more than one person. A child can learn how to attach as a preschooler. Recent research suggests that people can change the security of their attachment style well into adulthood, and that is the whole foundation for this guidebook.

LOVE AND ATTACHMENT: A THEORY EMERGES

As the previous sections have illustrated, our need for relationships and attachment is as basic as food and housing. It is not a luxury, but an important element we really need. So how can it be that some people in this world feel lonely and have nobody in their lives? This is a sad and extreme problem, as serious as poverty where people have no food or a roof to protect them. For the most part, people do have relationships. The common experience is that they are not satisfying or they are the cause of their pain. The problem is about the *quality*.

I would like to share a statement that best illustrates the world we live in today, summarized by Mother Theresa's final words before she died. When she was asked what worried her most about the future of the western world, she said: LONELINESS. "There is hunger for ordinary bread, and there is hunger for love, for kindness, for thoughtfulness; and this is the great poverty that makes people suffer." What did she mean by that?

For a long time, powerful influences from society and even from the psychological field have promoted independence, strength, self-reliance, lack of emotional expression and fast solutions (give me a pill.) Unfortunately, this is what most of us consider or describe as "normal." Furthermore, in the current world we have fewer and fewer opportunities to develop close relationships. We don't tend to live as close to our families or early childhood neighbourhoods as our grandmothers used to. We work and commute longer hours, we move many times, leaving people behind, we change jobs frequently to advance our careers, and so forth. Therefore, rates of depression, suicide, mental illness, and divorce continue to grow even though the field of medical science is better than in the past.

Likewise, in the latest survey of the National Science Foundation in 2006, couples reported that they live in a community of two most of the time, and more people reported that they had no one at all to confide in. This survey shows how we now ask one or two people for the fulfilment and support that our grandparents used to get from a whole community. The most interesting aspect is that despite all these facts, more people in the USA and Canada rated a satisfying relationship as their number one goal. So even though everything we are doing promotes loneliness and independence we still want intimacy and attachment deep down. WE WANT LOVE!

WHAT IS LOVE?

So what do we mean by love? I cannot assume to propose final conclusions in this project, but it is my humble desire to provide you with the basic understanding of what we know so far. "Only a few things worth knowing about love can be proven, and just a few things amenable to proof are worth knowing at all." (Lewis, et al, 2001)

According to what we know so far, love is more than an indefinable powerful emotion. Research on adult attachment is guided by the assumption that the same motivational system that gives rise to the close emotional bond between parents and their children is responsible for the bond that develops between adults in emotionally intimate relationships.

Many scientists, poets and people in general have tried throughout the years to define love but conclude it is a universal, powerful, and illogical emotion that is impossible to define as it is different and unique for everyone. Aversely, Susan Johnson, PhD. (2008) emphasizes that today we can't afford to continue defining love as an indefinable construct. It is imperative that we comprehend what love is, how to make it and how to make it last. She affirms that adult romantic love is an attachment bond that lives deep in primordial pathways in the brain. Love is not the least bit illogical or random, but actually an ordered and wise recipe for survival. We now have a map that can guide us in creating, healing and sustaining love.

"Grounded in science, it reveals that love is vital to our existence. And far from being unfathomable, love is exquisitely logical and understandable. What's more, it is adaptive and functional. Even better, it is malleable repairable, and durable." (Johnson, et al, 2013)

If we understand the exquisite logic of love, we can understand how to make it healthy, nurturing, and rewarding, and we can heal from the wounds that love, impaired by unhealthy attachment, inflicts.

LOVE AS A SURVIVAL NEED

"We have a wired-in need for emotional contact and responsiveness from significant others. It's a survival response, the driving force of the bond of security a baby seeks with its mother. This observation is at the heart of attachment theory. A great deal of evidence indicates that the need for secure attachment never disappears; it evolves into the adult need for a secure emotional bond with a partner. Think of how a mother lovingly gazes at her baby, just as two lovers stare into each other's eyes." (Johnson, et al, 2008)

Love is the most powerful compelling survival mechanism of the human species. It does not exist only for the purpose of reproduction (since we can manage to do that without love) but because of the bond and attachment that produces the nourishment and security that we all need to be alive and face the world every day.

The need to be loved is wired into our genes and our bodies. It is as basic to life, health and happiness as food, shelter, and sex. We need to be emotionally attached to others to be physically and emotionally healthy, to survive (Johnson, et al, 2008). Many studies have shown that both the quality and quantity of social connections have an impact on our health and longevity as well as our psychological wellbeing. A good relationship, says psychologist Bert Uchino of the University of Utah, is the single best recipe for good health and the most powerful antidote to aging. He notes that twenty years of research with thousands of subjects shows how the quality of our social support predicts general mortality as well as mortality from specific disorders, such as heart disease. (Johnson, et al, 2013)

So why is it that we are used to hearing common statements like the ones below and think they are ok?

"I am ok alone."

"I am supposed to be ok alone because if not, I am too needy."

"You need to love yourself first before loving anybody else."

"I have not found the right one yet."

"Being independent is a sign of being stronger."

Can you identify with one or more of these statements? Let me tell you that these are false beliefs people in our modern society had to create in order to survive. It is a rationalization, not the truth. These false beliefs act in the same way dissociation occurs with abuse or neglect. In societies like America, the values of independence and financial success are overvalued and they interfere with the development of love and families. In a seventy five year study, one of the longest running longitudinal studies of human development, Harvard researchers uncovered the one true key to a happy existence: love. Lead researcher Dr. George Vaillant even concluded that relationships are the only thing that really matter.

This is why all of this is so important! Today attachment theory is the main theory that describes love and contributes to the explanation of many other benefits such as resilience and emotional balance. One of the major tenets of attachment theory is the idea that an infant's early attachment pattern can have long-term developmental effects. Our attachment influences not only the relationships we rely on, but also broader aspects of behaviour such as levels of anxiety, levels of aggression, stress management skills, resilience and social interactions. For our purposes, we will focus on understanding the basics of adult Attachment and its implications in our relationships.

CHAPTER TWO

My Attachment Style

AN INTRODUCTION TO ATTACHMENT STYLES AND HOW THEY DEVELOP

As I mentioned in the beginning, there are internal factors such as genetics, medical conditions, and other aspects outside of our control which can play an important role in our relationships. For these factors, there is nothing we can do but follow our doctor's directions or treatment; addressing these factors is not the purpose of this guidebook. If a person has a genetic or mental condition, keeping that in check will involve a more complex medical and psychological treatment at both a personal and relational level. We are here to focus on the environmental or relational patterns which define our relationships, patterns that we are able to change with awareness and dedication.

What are relational patterns? Relational patterns are the set of common behaviors, feelings and expectations that develop as a result of our relationship history and attachment systems. In other words, our previous relational experiences influence our present and future relationships.

Bolwby proposed that from infancy to adolescence, individuals gradually build up expectations of attachment based on experiences with attachment figures. Main expectations revolve around the availability and responsiveness of attachment figures and are then incorporated into "internal working models" (subconscious thoughts) which guide perceptions and behavior in later relationships. (Feeney, 2007)

Although some people are extremely fortunate and were raised by two happy, healthy parents who had great communication and relational skills, many of us were not as fortunate and did not develop healthy relational patterns when we were young. Research shows that about 50% of the general population has an insecure attachment. Therefore the probability of succeeding in relationships without extra work is close to 50/50.

According to Bowlby, "Virtually all children - if given any opportunity at all - become attached, but the quality of attachment varies widely." (as cited in Cassidy and Mohr, 2001)

During the past two decades since Hazan & Shaver's (1987) seminal papers when romantic love started to be conceptualized as an attachment process, hundreds of scientific studies in a wide range of countries have carefully delineated the ways in which adults behave in romantic ties. Understanding these styles is an easy and reliable way to understand and predict people's behavior in romantic situations. One of the most fascinating aspects of attachment research is the discovery that people with different attachment styles perceive situations in different and often opposing manners. They pay attention to different aspects of situations and they interpret them differently. Even their brain activity can be remarkably different.

Gaining insight into adult attachment styles is akin to a having a road map to romantic behavior, not only to others' but also to your own.

ATTACHMENT STARTS IN INFANCY

As we have already defined it, attachment is "the result of the bonding process that occurs between a child and caregiver during the first couple years of the child's life." The first year of life is the year of needs. The infant's primary needs are touch, eye contact, movement, smiles, and nourishment. When the infant has a need, he or she expresses the need through crying. Ideally, the caretaker is able to recognize and satisfy the need. Through this interaction, which occurs hundreds of thousands of times in a year, the child learns that the world is a safe place and trust develops.

In addition, emotional connection forms. The child feels empowered in his or her environment and develops a secure base from which to confidently explore the world and trust other people. Attachment is reciprocal; the baby and caregiver create this deep, nurturing connection together. It takes two to connect. It is imperative for optimal brain development and emotional health, and its effects are felt physiologically, emotionally, cognitively and socially.

Attachment bond theory states that the relationship between infants and primary caretakers is responsible for (Segal & Jaffe, 2015) sustain:

- shaping our future relationships
- strengthening or damaging our abilities to focus, to be conscious of our feelings, and to calm ourselves (internal emotional

regulation)

- forming our ability to bounce back from misfortune: resilience

When this initial attachment is lacking, children lack the ability to form and maintain loving, intimate relationships. They grow up with an impaired ability to trust that the world is a safe place and that others will take good care of them. Without this sense of trust, children believe that they must be hyper vigilant about their own safety. Unfortunately, their idea of safety is often skewed and prevents them from allowing others to take care of them in a loving, nurturing manner. They become extremely demanding and controlling in response to their fear. Emotionally they believe that if they do not control their world, they will die.

THE ROOTS OF IMPAIRED ATTACHMENT

Children without proper care in the first few years of life have unusually high levels of stress hormones which adversely affect the way crucial aspects of the brain and body develop. Conscience development is dependent upon brain development. Healthy brain develops under low levels of stress and high levels of security and connection, which are also the main ingredients for healthy attachment.

What happens when infant and caregiver attachment behaviors are consistently less than optimal? Insecure attachment occurs. Insecure attachment is adaptive and happens when caregivers are generally unavailable and rejecting which causes infants to develop internal representations of themselves as unworthy and unlovable. The typical exploratory and comfort seeking behavior of securely attached children may lead to discomfort in some parents. These behaviors reflect the fact that the child has learned over time the type of behavior they must exhibit in order to most likely elicit the needed response from their parents. In cases of severely disrupted attachment, children can lack social values and morality, sometimes demonstrating aggressive, disruptive and antisocial behaviors.

Insecure attachment is not psychopathology, but it is a risk factor for it.

By now you may be thinking: "Oh boy...this sounds so extreme! I know this did not happen to me. I grew up in a caring, loving family, so this is not *my* case." It is true- most people haven't experienced the extreme circumstances described above. But if you are reading this guide, something happened somehow and in some ways wasn't optimal. Can you identify with any of the points below? These can help to indicate if your relational patterns are preventing you from having a healthy relationship:

- You find yourself attracted to the same type of person again and again, even though in the end, the dynamic never works out
- You start and finish all new relationships practicing the same behavioral patterns that you did with all previously failed relationships (getting too close too fast, cutting off the other person, being too private or disclosing too much)
- Most or all of your intimate relationships follow the same course

throughout the relationship- same or similar problems, same or similar resolution

- You are convinced that it is not you who is contributing to the failed relationship- it's the other person, every time
- Changing your behavioral or cognitive patterns seems impossible, even when they are not helping you to get what you want
- Your behavioral and cognitive patterns are extremely black or white, lacking grey or something in between
- Your family and friends frequently make comments that suggest you may have negative relational patterns

There are some extremely unfortunate cases where things go mostly wrong for an individual and their attachment style is drastically compromised. The difference for the majority of people is that though most of the significant things went well, some things still went wrong in a subtle way at an attachment level. That is why they are healthy and functional most of the time and their life is good in many aspects. The struggle may come mostly from what I call a "vitamin deficiency" or a crack in the foundation. They received nurturing and care but it wasn't in a consistent enough way or in the ways or doses they needed it to be. If you are struggling in your current relationship, some things didn't go well *enough*, and therefore, we need to supplement.

Here some of the many reasons why the development of the attachment connection can be disrupted, from dramatic cases to the more subtle ones:

- Intergenerational attachment difficulties
- Lack of fit with parent
- Child's temperament
- Premature birth
- In-utero trauma such as exposure to drugs or alcohol
- Unwanted pregnancy
- Separation from birth mother
- Postpartum depression or other mental conditions of the mother and/or caretakers
- Genetic disorders: family history of mental illness, depression, aggression, criminality, substance abuse, antisocial personality
- Violence and poverty
- Lack of support (absent father or extended kin, lack of services, isolation)
- High stress (marital conflict, family disorganization and chaos, violent community)
- Lack of stimulation
- Over worked parents
- Abuse and/or neglect in the first years of life (isolation or loneliness)
- Multiple caretakers (continuous succession of nannies or daycare staff in short periods of time)

- Frequent moves or placements- constantly changing environments (for example, children who spend their early years in foster care, children in military or diplomat families etc.)
- Hospitalizations
- Unresolved pain
- Painful or invasive medical procedures
- Insensitive or inexperienced parenting
- Cold or distant parenting (lack of empathy for and language about feelings; lack of emotional presence and validation)
- Role reversal (the child is mostly taking care of their parent's emotions; the parent is the priority instead of the child's own needs and wants)
- Intrusive, over-anxious parents
- Most common and subtle: the parent's own insecure attachment and unresolved trauma history.

When any of the above situations happen, children can learn at a pre-verbal stage that the world is not a safe enough place and that they cannot fully trust people. This lesson takes place at a biochemical level in the brain. But have hope! We have learned so much more about the brain and attachment in recent years. The good news is that attachment is not set in stone. Though it is true that the first year and first relationships are extremely significant in creating the foundation for future ones to come, attachment is influenced and changeable both ways. If we have had difficult relationships as children but have healthier and more lovable experiences later in life, we can heal and lean towards secure attachment. The opposite is also true: we can have had secure attachment in our early life, but if we have an unhealthy partner or traumatic experiences later on, we can develop an insecure attachment later in life as well. An insecure attachment developed later in life is easier to reverse as earlier traumas are more complex, but the most important thing to remember is that we can change it and therefore we can improve it.

DETERMINING MY OWN ATTACHMENT STYLE!

As you may have guessed by now, there are different types of attachment depending on the quality of main relationships throughout life: the secure or optimally healthy attachment and various types of insecure attachment (which are the focus of this guide!) Each attachment style has different ways of manifesting and relating. I would like to emphasize at this point that attachment style struggle is not a diagnosis or a mental illness. Every person, whether he or she just started dating or has been married for forty years, falls into one of the attachment style categories. Dr. Phillip Shaver and Dr. Cindy Hazan (2010) found that about 60 percent of people have a secure attachment, while 20 percent have an avoidant attachment, and 20 percent have an anxious attachment.

I would also like to emphasize that the attachment style you developed as a child based on your relationship with a parent or early caretaker doesn't have to define your ways of relating to those you love in your adult life. Coming to know your attachment style will help you uncover ways you are defending yourself from getting close and being emotionally connected. You will gain insight into how you felt and emotionally developed in your childhood. You will also see the ways in which you are emotionally limited as an adult and understand what you can change to improve your close relationships, including your relationship with your own children.

To get the most advantage from attachment theory, you need to know what your attachment style is. Keep in mind that because styles are fluid and not "all or nothing", you might present characteristics of more than one style, including some secure traits. Focus on the one that is the most prominent.

This exercise will help you to determine your predominant attachment style!

EXERCISE: Pin-Pointing My Attachment Style

There is a variety of attachment questionnaires out there. Most tests are short and absolute, as they are supposed to be for their purposes, but I feel that a lot of people don't relate to them. I have prepared an exercise with a slightly different and more relaxed approach. The following are statements which reflect the different attachment styles. Instead of working towards a determinant score, you and/or your partner can simply read through them and see which ones describe you best or which combination you identify with most fully. This is more of a "food for thought" curiosity-inspired exploration entry. The purpose here is to start to uncover more of your complex psychological reality and begin to widen your awareness. I will direct you to a fully validated questionnaire later on for those readers who are interested.

Mark on the right any statement that feels somewhat or very true to you. Don't worry about the degree:

1. I feel open to explore and reflect on my own attachment situation right now.
2. I feel people are essentially good at heart.
3. I feel the world is, in general, a safe place.
4. If I had to choose, I would prefer to do something with people/partner rather than something I enjoy alone.
5. If I had to choose, I would prefer to do something I enjoy by myself rather than a social activity or with my partner, for the most part.
6. For the most part, my work and hobbies interfere with my family and social life.
7. I tend to show love by providing.
8. I prefer to not depend on people.
9. It is relatively easy for me to get close to people and my partner.
10. It is very important for me to be independent.

11. I worry people will often hurt me and disappoint me if I get too close.

12. I usually like it when things progress fast in my relationships.

13. I am comfortable without emotionally close relationships.

14. I am comfortable depending on other people.

15. I don't feel comfortable when others want or get too close to me.

16. I am comfortable when other people depend on me.

17. I often feel people are never there when you need them.

18. I worry about being alone.

19. I often worry about not having enough time for myself.

20. I often worry that others don't value me or love me as much as I value or love them.

21. I think it is "not ok" when other people want to know more about me or want to get too close.

22. I find that others aren't as open or would not like to get as close as I would like sometimes.

23. I trust that others will be there when I need them.

24. I trust that even when things aren't great, things will be ok in my relationship and my partner loves me.

25. When things are bad in my relationship I try to distract myself, not think, and do something else.

26. When things are bad in my relationship I try to talk things over and don't stop until we resolve them.

27. Romantic partners usually want more from me.

28. I am usually the one that gives more in the relationship.

29. It is easier for me to think things through than to express myself emotionally.

30. I often expect things to go wrong in my relationship.

31. I tend to spend a lot of time with things or animals.

32. I second-guess myself frequently.

33. I tend to feel guilty if I put myself first or take care of my needs.

34. I have difficulty reaching out when I need help and do many of life's tasks and solve my problems alone.

35. I am usually yearning for something or someone that I feel I cannot have and rarely feel satisfied.

36. If I get upset I find it difficult to continue to perform daily life tasks such as work, sleep or taking care of myself.

37. When under stress I pride myself for keeping calm and focus on the problem to solve.

38. When I reach a certain level of intimacy with my partner, I sometimes experience inexplicable fear.

39. I have a hard time remembering and discussing the feelings related to my past attachment situations. I disconnect or dissociate and get confused.

40. I look at my partner with kindness and caring and look forward to our time together.

41. I find myself making the effort to put things aside to be with people or my partner.

42. I find myself sometimes putting my life aside too often in order to be with my family or partner.

43. I feel like other people in my life sometimes put their needs aside in order for me to get my needs met.

44. I feel like not many people in my life sometimes put their needs aside in order for me to get my needs met.

45. I feel guilty most of the time if other people sacrifice for me to get what I want or to get my needs met.

46. I think I have a healthy balance of time alone and time with people/my partner.

47. I feel a deep wish to be close but always find a reason why I can't make the next step.

48. I can keep secrets, protect my partner's privacy, and respect boundaries.

49. I find myself minimizing the importance of close relationships in my life.

50. I want to be close with my partner but feel angry at my partner at the same time.

51. I feel like I over-focus on others in general and tend to lose myself in relationships.

52. I struggle to trust my partner and people in general.

53. It is difficult for me to say NO or to set realistic boundaries.

54. When I lose a relationship I feel scared and become depressed.

55. I act like I don't need reassurance or encouragement when sometimes I do.

56. When my partner arrives home or approaches me, I feel inexplicably stressed - especially when s/he wants to connect.

57. It is a priority to keep agreements with my partner.

58. I often find eye contact uncomfortable and particularly difficult to maintain.

59. I feel like my partner is always there but I would often prefer to have my own space unless I invite the connection.

60. I am often told by my partner that I don't give enough, or I feel that they are too needy.

61. I often feel that my partner isn't actually present with me or that there is not enough going on.

62. I am stuck in approach-avoidance patterns with my partner; I want closeness but am also afraid of it.

63. When I give more than I get, I usually don't mind at the beginning but after a while I often resent this and feel used.

64. It is difficult to receive love from my partner when they express it.

65. It is difficult for me to be alone. If I'm alone, I feel abandoned, hurt, and angry.

66. Most of the time I prefer casual sex instead of a committed relationship.

67. My partner often comments or complains that I am not loving/connected/involved enough.

68. If my partner and I hit a glitch it is relatively easy for me to apologize, brainstorm a win-win solution, or repair the mis-attunement or disharmony.

69. I am more prone to feeling sorry for myself when I have a problem than to take action and solve it.

70. I am comfortable being affectionate with my partner and receiving affection from him/her.

71. I attempt to discover and meet the needs of my partner whenever possible and I feel comfortable expressing my own needs.

Now look at the table below and mark with and "S," (secure) "AX (Anxious), or "AV" (Avoidant) the statements you selected according to their number.

1 S 2 S 3S 4 S/AX 5 AV 6 AV 7 AV 8 AV 9 S/AX 10 AV 11 AV 12 AX 13 AV 14 S/AX 15 AV 16 S/AX 17AX 18 AX 19AV 20AX 21AV 22AX 23 S 24 S 25 AV 26 AX 27 AX 28 AX 29 AV 30 AX 31 AV 32 AX 33AX 34 AV 35 AX 36 AX 37 AV 38AV 39 AV 40 S 41 S 42 AX 43 S 44 AX 45 AX 46 S 47 AV 48 S 49 AV 50 AX 51 AX 52 AX 53 AX 54 AX 55 AV 56 AV 57 S 58 AV 59 AV 60 AV 61 AX 62AV 63 AX 64 AV 65 AX 66 AV 67 AV 68 S 69 AX 70 S/AX 71 S

For a fully validated adult attachment questionnaire, you can log on to Dr. Chris Fraley's website at: http://www.web-research-design.net/cgi-bin/crq/crq.pl.

Now that you have your test results, we will deepen your understanding of your attachment style(s) by understanding the four patterns of adult attachment.

THE DIFFERENT STYLES OF ATTACHMENT

There are 3 types of insecure attachment styles: Anxious (Ambivalent), Avoidant (Dismissive) and a sub-category called Disorganized (Fearful).

Here is a graphic that shows the dimensions of attachment. If you completed Dr. Fraley's web test, the results will show you which quadrant you are in and how low or high you fall in terms of each tenure. If you aren't sure where you are in the diagram, it is probably because you have a combination of styles, which is pretty common. The key is to see how high or low you are in terms of anxiety and avoidance.

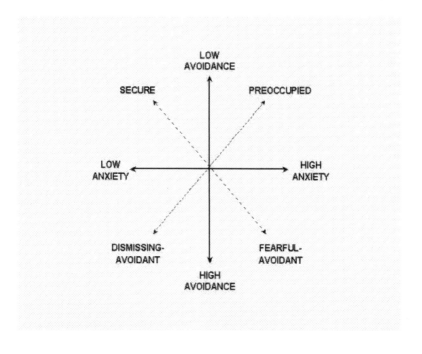

Figure 1. Two dimensional model of adult attachment (Fraley & Shaver, 2004)

Bowlby claims that attachment patterns reflect unconscious working models (concepts or thoughts) of self and others. The following chart explains this concept in more detail:

	Secure	**Avoidant**	**Anxious**	**Fearful**
View of Self	Worthy of love and attention	Worthy of love or attention	Unworthy of love or attention	Unworthy of love or attention
View of Others	See others as trustful and available.	Trust others but see them as too available.	Trust others but see them as unavailable.	Distrust others and sees them as unavailable.
Love Characteristics	High on intimacy, passion, and commitment	Low on intimacy, passion, and commitment	High on intimacy, passion, and commitment	Low on intimacy, passion, and commitment
	Comfortable with interdependence (intimacy & autonomy)	Denial of Attachment Needs Counter dependent. Achievement & Self-Reliance at expense of intimacy. Avoids closeness for fear of losing control/autonomy	Desires Attachment Dependent Intimacy & Acceptance at expense of autonomy. Excessive fear of rejection or abandonment	Wants intimacy but distrust others. Dependent / Counter dependent Social insecurity, need of approval, lack of assertiveness. Avoids closeness

				for fear of loss or rejection.

Figure 2. The four adult attachment styles defined by Bartholomew in terms of working models of self and others. From Bartholomew (1990). Copyright by Sage Publications, Inc. Reprinted with permission.

To enhance your understanding of how these styles manifest for an individual, the following is a list of the main traits for the most common insecure styles, Avoidant and Anxious (Evergreen Consultants in Human Behavior, 2013). It can help you identify yourself, a parent or partner(s). Keep in mind that some people might present more traits than others or traits from different styles:

AVOIDANT

- Intense sense of anger and loss
- Hostile
- Critical of others
- Sensitive to blame
- Lack of empathy
- Views others as untrustworthy
- Views others as undependable
- Views self as unlovable or "too good" for others
- Relationships feel either threatening to one's sense of control, not worth the effort, or both

- Compulsive self-reliance
- Passive withdrawal
- Low levels of perceived support
- Difficulty getting along with co-workers, often preferring to work alone
- Uses work as a good excuse to avoid personal relations
- Fear of closeness in relationships
- Avoidance of intimacy to satisfy needs for autonomy
- Places greater weight on goals such as achievement
- Unlikely to idealize the love relationship
- Not interpersonally oriented
- Manage distress by cutting off anger
- Minimize distress-related emotional displays; withhold intimate disclosure
- Need to maintain distance
- Tendency toward introjective depression (self critical)

ANXIOUS

- Compulsive care giving
- Feels over involved and underappreciated
- Rapid relationship breakups
- Idealizing of others
- Strong desire for partner to reciprocate in relationship
- Desire for extensive contact and declarations of affections
- Over invests his/her emotions in a relationship

- Perceives relationships as imbalanced
- Relationship is idealized
- Preoccupation with relationship
- Dependence on relationship
- Heavy reliance on partner
- Views partner as desirable but unpredictable (sometimes available, sometimes not)
- Perceives others as difficult to understand
- Relationship is the primary method by which one can experience a sense of security
- Unlikely to view others as altruistic
- Sensitive to rejection
- Discomfort with anger
- Extreme emotions
- Jealous
- Possessive
- Views self as unlovable
- Suicide attempts
- Mood swings
- Tendency toward anaclitic depression (dependent depression)

ATTACHMENT STYLES IN RELATIONSHIPS

According to international expert on relationships, Lisa Firestone, PhD (2013), founder and director of the Glendone Association since

1987, most people behave in relationships according to their attachment style. This is how:

> ***Secure Attachment*** – Securely attached adults tend to be more satisfied in their relationships. Children with a secure attachment see their parent as a secure base from which they can venture out and independently explore the world. A secure adult has a similar relationship with their romantic partner, feeling secure and connected, while allowing themselves and their partner to move freely.
>
> Secure adults offer support when their partner feels distressed. They also go to their partner for comfort when they themselves feel troubled. Their relationship tends to be honest, open and equal, with both people feeling both independent and loving.
>
> ***Anxious Attachment*** – Unlike securely attached couples, people with an anxious attachment tend to be desperate to form a fantasy bond. Instead of feeling real love or trust toward their partner, they often feel emotional hunger. They are frequently looking to their partner to rescue or complete them. Although they're seeking a sense of safety and security by clinging to their partner, they take actions that push their partner away.
>
> Even though anxiously attached individuals act desperate or insecure, more often than not, their behavior exasperates their own fears. When they feel unsure of their partner's feelings and unsafe in their relationship they often become clingy,

demanding or possessive toward their partner. They may also interpret independent actions by their partner as affirmation of their fears. For example, if their partner starts socializing more with friends, they may think, "See? He doesn't really love me. This means he is going to leave me. I was right not to trust him."

Avoidant Attachment – People with a dismissive avoidant attachment have the tendency to emotionally distance themselves from their partner. They may seek isolation and feel "pseudo-independent," taking on the role of parenting themselves. They often come off as focused on themselves and may be overly attentive to their creature comforts. Pseudo-independence is an illusion, as every human being needs connection. Nevertheless, people with a dismissive avoidant attachment tend to lead more inward lives, both denying the importance of loved ones and detaching easily from them. They are often psychologically defended and have the ability to shut down emotionally. Even in heated or emotional situations, they are able to turn off their feelings and not react. For example, if their partner is distressed and threatens to leave them, they would respond by saying, "I don't care; you can do whatever you want."

Disorganized Attachment – A person with a disorganized attachment lives in an ambivalent state of being afraid of being both too close to and too distant from others. They attempt to keep their feelings at bay but are unable to. They can't just avoid their anxiety or run away from their feelings. Instead, they are overwhelmed by their reactions and often experience emotional storms. They tend to be mixed up or unpredictable in their moods. They see their relationships from the working model that you need to go towards others to get your needs met, but if you get close to others, they will hurt you. In other words, the person they want to go to for safety is the same person they are frightened to be close to. As a result, they have no organized strategy for getting their needs met by others.

As adults, these individuals tend to find themselves in rocky or dramatic relationships, with many highs and lows. They often have fears of being abandoned but also struggle with being intimate. They may cling to their partner when they feel rejected, then feel trapped when they are close. Oftentimes, the timing seems to be off between them and their partner. A person with fearful avoidant attachment may even wind up in an abusive relationship.

Now let's look at what happens when different attachment styles match with one another.

Two people with a secure attachment style in a relationship is ideal. Those are the couples that we see and we say "how come it is so easy for them?" They get along so naturally, they are happy most of the time and when they fight they know how to solve the conflict without long-term negative consequences for the relationship.

How do these combinations happen? Romantic attachment studies have revealed a degree of "partner matching" based on our own working models (the lens through which we look at the world and other people). Secure individuals tend to be paired with secure, responsive partners (Cassidy & Shaver, Handbook of Attachment, 2010) - a situation that confirms the power of the subconscious.

What happens when less secure attachment styles "match"? Two avoidant styles may seem to be quite stable, although not necessarily very happy (Cassidy & Shaver, et al, 2010). This combination makes the typical couple who live separate lives.

The most typical combination in insecure attachment styles is one partner with avoidant style and the other with anxious style, which creates the common avoidant-pursuer dance. Presumably the clingy, anxious female confirms the avoidant male's belief that it is unwise to let others get too close, and the avoidant male confirms the anxious female's belief that others are distant and unsupportive. Even though gender is not a determinant in these types of combinations, this is the most common combination seen in couples' therapy.

Individuals with avoidant and anxious attachment styles are more likely to experience relational dissatisfaction (Shaver & Mikulincer, 2007). Here is a summary of the reasons according to each style:

Avoidant Style

- Possible previous negative view of relationships in regard to trust and intimacy (Bartholomew & Horowitz, 1991)

- Avoidance directly predicts levels of relational hostility (attachment theory suggests that avoidant individuals eschew intimacy and disengage from partners, both of which are characteristics Gottman uses to describe people in hostile relationships- more covert hostility)
- Less validating behaviors in the relationship
- Lack of engagement, emotionally and physically

Anxious Style

Anxiety may have less of an impact than avoidance on relationship satisfaction. Perhaps this is because avoidance is a behavior while anxiety is more of a feeling.

- Presence of high levels of emotional distress and cognitive preoccupation with loss or distancing
- Jealousy
- More validating
- Engage in high conflict and emotional arguments. More overt hostility.

Disorganized

- Mostly a combination of the above. *I will not be covering this attachment style as the previous two because to understand disorganized attachment you need to understand trauma. Therefore, it requires more professional personal help!*

Now since life is not completely black and white, there are exceptions to these trends. As we mentioned earlier, about 50% of the general population has an insecure attachment style. This means that there is a wide variety of combinations: some of them produce high levels of conflict or dissatisfaction, a few complement each other, and some produce a combination of both effects.

For example, if someone with an insecure attachment gets together with a person with a secure attachment, there are probabilities for the relationship to be ok because the person with secure attachment can counterbalance the needs or insecurities of the other partner.

> "I had a real problem trusting anyone at the start of any relationship. A couple of things happened to me when I was young, which I had some emotional difficulties getting over. At the start of our relationship, if P had been separated from me I would have been constantly thinking, 'What is he doing?' 'Was he with another girl?' 'Was he cheating on me?'- all that would have been running through my head. Over a 3-year period of going out, you look at it in a different light; you learn to trust him." Excerpt from study (Cassidy & Shaver, 2008, p.465)

On the other hand, a person with secure attachment may become insecure as a result of various experiences:

> "Before I started seeing T, I was in another long relationship with another fellow…It was good up until about 10 months, and the last couple of months were really bad. I was always really

confident about myself and secure about myself, but how he made me feel in 2 months - just seemed to ruin everything. I'd never felt good about myself, and I felt bad about everything. So now, I've got this constant thing in the back of my head that maybe this will happen again." (Cassidy & Shaver, et al, p.466)

The problem is that more often than not, two people with insecure attachment get together because working models are also self-perpetuating. For example, someone who believes that others are untrustworthy may approach them defensively, eliciting further rejection.

Let's look at more examples to illustrate how the styles manifest in daily real life interactions Extracts from reports of Romantic Relationship Research (Cassidy & Shaver, et al, p. 360):

Secure: "We are really good friends and we sort of knew each other for a long time before we started going out. Another thing I like is that he gets on well with my close friends. We can always talk things over. Like if we are having any fights, we usually resolve them by talking it over. He's a very reasonable person. I can just be my own person and be open about my feelings and fears, so it's good, because I am never afraid of things not resolving. I think that we trust each other a lot."

Avoidant: "My partner is my best friend, and that's the way I think of her. She's one of the most special people in my life. I do not know if her expectations in life include marriage, or any long-term commitment, which is fine with me because that's not one of my priorities anyway. I like that we are very independent people and we support our own goals and respect each other's autonomy, which is good. Sometimes it worries me that a person can be that close to you and want to control your life. I have dated people like that and I couldn't do it."

Anxious: "So I went in there… and he was sitting on the bench, and I took one look, and I actually melted. He was the best-looking thing I'd ever seen, and that was the first thing that struck me about him. So we went out and we had lunch in the park… So we just sort of sat there in silence but it wasn't awkward. We just sat there, and it was incredible, like we'd known each other for a real long time, and we'd only known each other for a few days. So that was it. I knew since that moment that we were meant to be."

Joyce S. Parker, PhD, a couple's therapist in Los Angeles, provides the following examples of how "Attachment Styles" can explain how you feel and behave in relationships. Let's look at Eli, Jen, Doris and Sergio- four adults, four different ways of handling important relationships:

Sergio gets along well in most relationships. He seems prepared to accept and give love, trust and partnership. He seldom has a hidden agenda or ends up in a fight with his partner.

Eli gets uncomfortable when a woman wants to get close: he seeks distance. He seems to value his intimate relationship less than his job, fantasy games, buddies or sports.

Jen's need for reassurance never ends. She is suspicious about her boyfriend's activities and obsessively worried that he might not truly love her. Her neediness, demands and accusations sometimes push partners away.

Doris doesn't know what she wants from her partner. She may be unable to leave an unhealthy or abusive situation. She suffers emotionally or physically, but is paralyzed by doubts and confusion. She often feels overwhelmed.

Can you guess by now which style each person presents?

Now that you have a deeper understanding of attachment styles, you may be wondering if it is possible to work towards a more secure attachment. The good news is- YES! The next chapter will begin this journey.

CHAPTER THREE

Deepening "Whole" Self Awareness Through Eight Parts

If your initial results were less than ideal, it doesn't mean that you have to continue to travel a path that isn't getting you where you want to go. In fact, research continues to show that the brain is changeable due to its capacity for neuroplasticity. This means that with awareness, effort and action, you can alter your path.

Unresolved childhood attachment issues leave an adult vulnerable to difficulties in forming secure adult relationships. Patterns of attachment tend to continue through the life cycle and across generations. New relations are affected by the expectations and unsatisfied needs from past relationships. There is a strong correlation between insecure adult attachment, marital dissatisfaction and negative couple interactions. If an adult does not feel safe with others, they will tend to be either rejecting of their partner or overly clingy.

Attachment problems are often handed down from one generation to the next unless someone breaks the chain. As a parent, an insecurely attached adult may lack the ability to form a strong attachment to their child and provide the necessary attachment cues required for the healthy emotional development of the child. This can predispose their child to a lifetime of relationship difficulties. With some awareness, work and dedication you will be able to break that chain.

When we can recognize knee-jerk memories, expectations, attitudes, assumptions and behaviors as problems resulting from insecure attachment bonds, we can end their influence on our adult relationships. That recognition allows us to reconstruct the healthy nonverbal communication skills that produce an attuned attachment and successful relationships.

In this section we will focus on some key strategies to help you "tune in" to your attachment style more deeply. Each part will lead you along a path to uncover, address, and reshape your internal working models by creating greater awareness in eight important areas.

In my experience, most people are willing to read books but not do the exercises. If you want to move your attachment style towards a more secure one, I encourage you to engage with these action steps from the start. Like anything else in life, you can't develop muscle or lose weight by reading a book or looking at pictures. You have to do something about it! Changing your relational patterns works in the same way.

PART ONE: AWARENESS OF MY CURRENT THOUGHTS, FEELINGS AND BEHAVIORS

The most noticeable moments for attachment style to manifest itself is during conflict. When people are under stress, they have less capacity to access the neurocortex and they react more spontaneously. Capturing how you react in stressful moments is a very useful tool for uncovering more about your attachment style. The following chart is a way for you to document this information. After selecting the ones that resonate with you, see if they fall closer to secure, avoidant, or anxious categories. The more you have under each category, the more prominent that style is for you.

EXERCISE: How I React When I am Under Stress/Conflict:

Check all the statements that reflect the way you feel or what you do when you are not in a good place:

What I Feel...

I feel scared

I feel afraid

I feel hurt

I feel vulnerable

I feel shut out or pushed away

I feel frustrated

I feel like getting back

I feel flooded with emotion

I feel hopeless

I feel isolated

I feel confused

I feel unable to calm myself

I feel abandoned

I feel like I can't let go

I feel misunderstood

I feel rejected

I feel wrong all the time

I feel invalidated

I feel angry

I feel guarded and closed up

I feel unable to think

I feel numb

I feel lonely/isolated

I feel sad

I feel unable to speak

I feel controlled

I feel unimportant

I feel I don't matter

I feel guilty

I feel powerless

I feel defeated

I feel blamed/attached

I feel criticized

I feel put down

I feel insignificant/don't matter

I feel intimidated

I feel dismissed

I feel empty

I feel ignored

I feel disconnected

I feel smothered

Try to figure out if you can also focus on your body:

I feel my body tense

I feel a knot in my throat

I feel pressure in my chest

I feel sick in my stomach

I feel like running

I feel like hitting Others....

What I Do:

I criticize

I withdraw

I scream

I close up

I get quiet

I rationalize

I defend

I blame

I attack

I leave

I play victim

I interrupt a lot

I don't listen

To help enhance your understanding of why you react the way you do, we can use the information you recorded here and pair it with the typical thoughts, feelings and behaviors of each style. For now, we will focus on the traits of the insecure attachment styles since those are the ones that we are trying to improve. The following charts show the most typical thoughts, feelings and behaviors of the two main insecure attachment styles, based on my experience and clinical observations:

Anxious Style Thoughts, Feelings, Behaviors

Thoughts	Feelings	Behaviors
Cathastrophizing: This is it. This will never get better. S/he's leaving me.	Abandoned	Pursues
	Sad/Depressed	Resorts to protest behavior
	Unappreciated	
All or nothing thinking: S/he will never call me again. See, s/he doesn't really care.	Resentful	Initiates communication most of the time
	Angry	
	Scared	Initiates fights or conflict
Generalizing: I will always be alone, nobody takes me seriously.	Unsettled	Wants to talk about emotions. Sometimes in an excessive way
	Rejected	
	Despaired	Shows affection, caring behaviors, and
	Hopeless	

Labeling: S/he is so selfish. All s/he thinks is about her/himself.	Lonely Irritated	physical touch most of the time Wants things done in a certain way
Fortune telling: I knew this was going to happen.	Jealous Guilty	Shows and provokes jealousy
Track keeping: This is the third time s/he does/doesn't do this. It's gotta stop! Taking it personally: It is because I said or did that. I totally ruined it. Inferiority complex: It is me again, there is	Defeated Overwhelmed Hateful Unlovable Negative / Pessimistic In love quickly and intensely Out of control	Tends to be open, generous and giving. Sometimes too much. Tends to alternate between aggressiveness and reactive passivity Reacts quickly. Sometimes act impulsively. Can be paralyzed and need a lot of external direction/ validation

something really wrong with me. I am way too needy and crazy. Superiority complex: What is wrong with him/her? Look at me. Why wouldn't s/he die to be with me? Revengeful: Oh you hurt me, fine! So now you are going to see/pay for it. Immediacy: I have to talk/to see him/her right now otherwise I can't be ok.	Loving Better than	Withdraw love when feeling hurt Keeps in mind/includes partner in personal life/activities. Sometimes in an excessive way.

Rumination tendencies: Can't stop thinking about it/s/he. Can't sleep or go back to work until things get resolved. Controlling: Maybe if I look really good next time we get back together…If I tell him/her what he/she wants to hear… If I make his/her favorite dinner… Fantasize: Remembering all the good things your partner ever did and said,		

focusing on all the good traits s/he has. Love knot: "If S/he loved me, s/he would…" Default thinking: "Let me show him/her how bad what s/he did so s/he works hard and changes it."		

Avoidant Typical Thoughts, Feelings, Behaviors

Thoughts	Feelings	Behaviors
Generalizing: Oh now s/he is going to be telling me what to do all the time, I am never going to see my friends or do my thing again. Labeling: S/he is too needy, something is wrong with him/her. Dismissive: When did that happen? Did I promise that? Oh it's not that bad...I was just busy. Taking it personally: I can never do anything right. No matter how	Shut down Indifferent Distrustful Hateful Resentful Aloof Engulfed In trouble Empty Restless Alone Misunderstood Frustrated Angry Deceived	Runs away Disconnect/deactivate behavior Avoids or doesn't initiate communication most of the time Stays away from fights or conflict in general Criticizes other's feelings or actions Denies and looks down on jealousy Tends to be self centered, withholding of affection. Doesn't initiate physical closeness.

much I try, s/he can never be happy.		Tends to alternate between passive-aggressive and dominant/controlling
Inferiority complex: I have to be my best at work, sports, and in shape so I don't have time for relationships.		Tends to take defensive position
		Keeps information and emotional sharing to a minimum. Sometimes too much.
Superiority complex: S/he has too many issues for me. I deserve and can get better.		Doesn't share feelings or emotions. Sticks to facts.
Self focused: If s/he can't accommodate/understand my needs I'd rather be on my own.		Tends to freeze and rejects external direction
		Withdraws loves when hurt
Minimizing tendencies: It is not so bad. I don't		

know why s/he is always so dramatic. Forgetful tendencies: I truly don't remember this being so important or you telling me. Blame: If you weren't nagging me all the time, things would be ok. Fantasize: If s/he was "the right one for me" we wouldn't fight so much. Relationships shouldn't be this hard, so we aren't meant to be. Also fantasize about having sex with other people.		

Typical Love knot: "If S/he was "the one," s/he...." Default thinking: "If things are so bad and I do things so wrong, then this relationship doesn't have any future."		

How many of each sounds familiar to you? Remember that attachment styles aren't firm or exclusive. You might have more aspects of one, which would be your predominant attachment style, but many times we tend to present traits of other styles as well.

PART TWO: AWARENESS OF MY EARLY ATTACHMENT EXPERIENCES

Each one of us has our own unique "story." In order to go deeper, you need to take some time for yourself, alone, to reflect on how your relational pattern developed. The answers lie in your earliest primary relationships and subconscious thoughts. Our history drives our behavior; to change our behavior we must first understand where it comes from and why we hold onto it, even when it makes us unhappy. This step requires some insight into the relationships with our parents, siblings and any other person that was significant during our upbringing. It is a difficult step because it usually requires breaking idealizations we had of those relationships and people. It also may involve grieving for: what we got or didn't get (positive and negative); direct and implied messages about ourselves, people, and the world; messages we didn't hear and we still crave for; what we were allowed and prohibited from; what was celebrated and what was punished, and so forth.

> *"Virtually all children- if given any opportunity at all- become attached, but the quality of attachment varies widely."*
>
> Bowlby, as quoted in Cassidy and Mohr, 2001

This step tends to be hard for people since most of us wonder what the point is of going over the past and criticizing our parents. This is not about criticizing our parents. Parental shortcomings are virtually all unintentional. Most parents love their children and are unaware that their behavior is having a negative impact. The reality of maternal love is true even for parents whose style causes a great deal of distress to their child. Going over our histories, even when it is painful and time consuming, is a crucial step in the beginning because we can only be compassionate and embrace what we understand, what we know.

As you do these exercises, remember that many of the issues that come up may not be a sign of bad parenting or intentions. Sometimes a parenting style and the child's temperament weren't compatible, even though on their own there was nothing intrinsically wrong with either one. I emphasize that because the purpose of this guidebook is to provide insight into common people's relationships dynamics; you don't need to have been abused or literally abandoned as a child to have intimacy problems. Your mom didn't need to be a victim of domestic violence, nor your dad an aggressive alcoholic. Dysfunction happens in the best families and in the most subtle ways. So it is important that you keep an open mind in the process. Focus on the ways you felt or reacted and not so much on the actual events of what did or did not happen.

Here there are three exercises that will help you start to deepen your insight about your early relationships experiences.

EXERCISE 1: CHILDHOOD WOUNDS

Time: Approximately 30 minutes

Purpose: This exercise is designed to refresh your memory of your caretakers and other influential people.

Directions:

Try to do some relaxing and breathing exercises to get you focused. When you are feeling peaceful, close your eyes and imagine your childhood home, the earliest one you can recall. Imagine yourself as a young boy or girl. Try to see the rooms from the perspective of a small child. Now wander around the house and find the people who influenced you most deeply as a child. As you encounter these people, you will be able to see them with new clarity. Stop and visit with each one. Note their positive and negative traits. Tell them what you enjoyed about being with them. Ex. Night time stories, delicious meals, help with homework… and what you didn't like about being with them. Ex: being criticized way too often, being compared with siblings, not being allowed personal opinions… Finally tell them what you wanted from them but never got. Ex: Be appreciated, receive expression of love, feel valued, accepted…Don't hesitate to share your angry, hurt, or sad feelings. In your fantasy, your caretakers will be grateful for your insights.

When you have gathered this information, open your eyes and record it according to the following instructions in the next exercise.

EXERCISE 2: IMAGO WORKUP- Based on Your Parents (we will be discussing your Imago more in the next section!)

Time: Approximately 30-45 minutes

Purpose: This exercise will help you record and summarize the information acquired in previous exercise.

Directions:

1. Take out a blank piece of paper and draw a large circle, leaving about 3 inches below the circle. Divide the circle in half with a horizontal line. Put a capital letter "B" above the line on the left side of the circle, and a capital letter "A" below the line of the left side of the circle. (See illustration below).

B
_____
A

2. On the top half next to the "B," list all the positive character traits of you mother, father, and any other people who influenced you strongly when you were young. Lump all the positive traits of all these people together (don't bother listing them individually). List these traits as you recall them from childhood. Do not describe your caretakers as they are today. Describe them with simple adjectives or phrases such as: "kind," "warm," "intelligent," "religious," "patient," "creative," "always there," "enthusiastic," "reliable," etc.

3. On the bottom half next to the "A," list the negative traits of these key people. Once again, lump all these traits together.

4. Circle the positive and negative traits that seem to affect you the most.

5. In the blank space below your circle, write down a capital "C" and complete this sentence: "What I wanted most as a child and didn't get was..."

6. Now write down a capital letter "D" and complete this sentence: "As a child, I had these negative feelings over and over again..."

(For the moment, ignore the capital letters. We will use them in one of the upcoming exercises.)

EXERCISE 3: CHILDHOOD FRUSTRATIONS

Time: Approximately 30-45 minutes

Purpose: This exercise will help you clarify your major childhood frustrations and describe the way you reacted to them.

Directions:

1. On a separate sheet of paper, list the recurrent frustrations you had as a child (see example below).

2. Next to the frustrations, briefly describe the way you reacted to the situations. (You may have responded in more than one way.

List all your common responses.) Put the capital letter "E" above your reactions as in the example.

Frustration	Response
Didn't get enough attention from my older brother	Was a pest. Kept trying to get his attention.
Father often gone	Sometimes I was angry. Usually tried to please him.
Felt inferior to older brother	Resigned myself to my inferiority. Tried not to compete directly.
My father drank too much	Tried to ignore it. Sometimes I would get stomachaches.
My mother was overly protective	I kept things to myself. Sometimes I was defiant.

Materials and exercises are a resource from *Getting the Love You Want* authored by Dr. Harville Hendrix and Dr. Helen LaKelly Hunt, 2001. More information available at imagorelationships.org

Another direct and easy way to find out about your childhood wounds is by exploring your most common frustrations in present relationships. Where there is enough pain or emotion there is usually an attachment wound. The following exercise will help you define these frustrations. We will expand on this exercise in later sections:

1. Typical Behavior(s):

   Ex: When you don't answer my questions...

2. Typical Feelings...

   Ex: Angry, sad, lonely, alienated, withdrawn, disappointed, rejected, trapped, irritated...

3. My Typical Reaction:

   Ex: Screaming, shutting down, nagging, withdrawing, pulling away ...

It is important with this exercise to be compassionate and accepting of yourself; your answers are what they are. We can wish they were different or that they didn't exist but we need to practice acceptance if we want healing to happen.

Another exercise I like is from PAIRS (Practical Application for Intimacy Relationships Skills Program, 1999) since it brings awareness about how some childhood patterns sneak into present adult relationships. It helps to bring understanding to our reactions in certain situations. I also like it because it focuses on us instead of what our partner's could change. In Chapter Four we will work on the last column and learn how we can choose more adaptive adult reactions in the future.

When.... happened	When I was a child I used to react by	As an adult, when my partner does.... I react by....	I would like to work on my new reaction being...*(You will be more ready to do this in Chapter Four)*
My father was angry and screamed and yelled	Going into my bedroom and withdrawing	When my partner is angry at me, I react by not wanting to talk	More open to discussing things, compromising on a certain day and time as long as there are not insults or screaming.
When I felt angry and expressed it, my mother told me that I was disrespectful	Feeling ashamed and repressing my feelings	When my partner is angry, I react by being judgmental and telling him/her he/she shouldn't be angry	Being more open to accept that anger is a normal feeling and working on a healthy expression of it from my partner and I.

PART THREE: AWARENESS OF MY IMAGO

Having a cohesive narrative about our lives is one of the main tenants of secure attachment. For this next part, we will deepen the concepts from Imago Theory by Dr. Harville Hendrix (1998). This powerful theory is based on childhood and the primary relationships we had with our parents. Its major thesis is that the purpose of the unconscious, in marital choices based on romantic attraction, is to finish childhood. Through this work you will gain information about your emotional and relational upbringing to complement your already-conscious factual and chronological history.

> "The Imago match is the determining factor in selection because it is driven by the unconscious purpose of recovering wholeness by restoring the connection, both personal and transpersonal, which was ruptured in childhood by need frustration. While the match between the positive and negative character traits and similar traits in the partner constitute the basis of attraction, the intensity of the attraction is a result of the match in negative traits – those connected to frustration."
> (Hendrix, 1998)

The Imago model states that "Romantic love is a creation of the unconscious mind." Imago is a concept that we have in our minds about our parents (or people who influenced us the most when we were a children) and it comes from the care that we received from them. It is based on the needs that were met and unmet during childhood. As adults, we go through life subconsciously looking for that Imago (*latin* term for "image"). Why? We unconsciously look for people with similar emotional traits as our primary caregivers or parents in order to resolve the unfinished business from our past. In other words, according to Hendrix, it is by getting our needs satisfied in the current relationship that we heal from the past and become complete. Or, from the perspective of attachment theory, this means that we earn a secure attachment style. Bingo!

You already began to uncover your Imago in your Imago Workup exercise on page 41. The following exercise will help you to uncover your "Imago" more clearly. Keep these sheets handy as we will use them later to look for any resemblance between your current partner and these earlier relationships.

EXERCISE 1: PRESENT PARTNER'S PROFILE

Time: Approximately 30-45 minutes

Purpose: This exercise will help you define the things you like and don't like about your partner and compare partner traits with Imago traits.

Directions:

1. On a separate sheet of paper, draw a large circle, leaving 3 inches of blank space below the circle. Divide the circle in half with a horizontal line. Put the capital letter "F" above the line on the left side of the circle. Put the capital letter "G" below the line on the left side of the circle.

F

G

2. On the top half of the circle (beside the "F") list your partner's positive traits. Include traits that first attracted you to your partner.

3. List your partner's negative traits beside the "G" on the lower half of the circle.

4. Circle the positive and negative traits that seem to affect you the most.

5. Now turn back to former exercise and compare your imago traits with your partner's traits. Star the traits that are similar.

6. On the bottom of the page, write the letter "H" and complete this sentence: "What I enjoy most about my partner is…"

7. Now write the letter "I" and complete this sentence: "What I want from my partner and don't get it…"

(Hendrix, et al, 1998)

This is your Imago!

Now, pull out your **Imago Workup** exercise from Part Two and see if there are any similarities. For some people the similarity between these two profiles is astonishing and for some people it's not so much. If your case is the second, it's no big deal; there are plenty of other exercises that might be more helpful in your case.

The discovery of your Imago can be very enlightening and freeing. Let me explain. In finding your Imago, you have found someone (I'm afraid) who is uniquely unqualified (at the moment) to give you the love you want. But at the same time this is what's supposed to happen! This explains why people with anxious attachment style tend to be attracted to people with avoidant attachment style, and vice versa. They've created what Levine & Heller (2010) call the "pursuer/avoidant trap" and what Hendrix calls the "power struggle." A lot of my clients think this is kind of depressing and I don't disagree, but hang in there- the good news is that there is a resolution. It is what is supposed to happen and, in the end, it is all for the better.

We all think that we have freedom of choice when it comes to selecting our partners. In a way, we do; ours are not arranged relationships after all. But regardless of what it is we think we're looking for in a mate, our unconscious has its own agenda. Levine & Heller think that interactions in relationships tend to be driven mostly by attachment reactions that we can't consciously control until we know what they are.

This is how it works:

The old brain has a mind of its own, with its own checklist of desired qualities. It is carrying around its own image of the perfect partner, a complex synthesis of qualities formed through our reactions to the way our caretakers responded to our needs. Every pleasure or pain, every transaction of childhood, has left its mark on us. These collective impressions form an unconscious picture that we're always trying to replicate as we scan our environment for a suitable mate.

This image of "the person who can make me whole again" is called the Imago. Though we consciously seek only the positive traits, the negative traits of our caretakers are more indelibly imprinted in our Imago picture because those are the traits which caused the wounds we now seek to heal. Our unconscious need is to have our feelings of aliveness and wholeness restored by someone who reminds us of our caretakers. In other words, we look for someone with the same deficits of care and attention that hurt us in the first place.

When we fall in love, when bells ring and the world seems altogether a better place, our old brain is telling us that we've found someone with whom we can complete our unfinished childhood business. But when the romantic love ends (illusion) the power struggle (realization that our needs are not going to be met but also that our partners are going to hurt us in the same way our parents did) begins. (Hendrix, et al., 1998)

Since we don't understand what's going on, when conflict begins or things don't go the way we expect, we tend to run screaming in the opposite direction. Most people do this, leaving relationship after relationship just to find another one with the same problems. This is because we are missing the point. It is precisely by two people learning to satisfy each other's needs that weren't met in the past that we can achieve a fulfilling relationship.

The more we know our stories and our partners' stories, the easier it is not judge, condemn or punish too quickly. We can become less harsh when dealing with annoying or painful current behaviors. Once you experience compassion, it is easier to embrace the person and their behavior or your own, and change can happen. Now that you know what is going on, you can change it by helping each other to move towards earning a secure attachment. This doesn't come naturally to us, and we have to learn it with time, effort and dedication. The benefits? It works, and is the best thing that can happen to anybody.

Conflict can have a purpose if we know how to survive it instead of becoming victims of it. Romantic love is supposed to end- initially it is the glue that bonds two incompatible people together so that they will do what needs to be done to heal themselves. If we remain fixated on romantic love, being "in love with love," we remain stuck at the one-year-old stage of attachment. To restore our wholeness, our relationships and each of us need to successfully grow through all the developmental stages that were mishandled during our childhood. We need to do our own personal work (by developing our child-adult self relationship and learning how to be more emotionally balanced) and work as a couple (by asking and responding to you and your partner's needs) to achieve this. If you don't have a partner, you may find great benefit in experiencing a healthy attachment relationship with a therapist.

Let's now find out if your attachment style tends to create a power struggle by being attracted to people that resemble your Imago. We will start by making a list of past intimate relationships. For each relationship, determine which characteristics you were attracted to as well as which traits you didn't like. Try to also include anything that started out on the attractive list but became annoying or even painful after awhile. Some of the traits might even move from one list to the other over time, or belong to both from the beginning.

Here a list of traits for you to use as guidance:

Intelligent	Caring	Volatile
Thinks outside the box	Courageous	Follow the rules
Different	Fun	Available
Unpredictable	Reliable	Consistent
Spontaneous	Powerful	Independent
Gentle	Vulnerable	Logical / Analytical
Practical	Romantic	Good looking / Beautiful
Attentive	Hardworking	Giving
Absent	Fragile	Scary
Strict	Cold	Mean
Unfair	Big picture	Detailed oriented
Generous	Conservative	Careful
Authoritarian	Empathic	Loyal
Use of eye contact	Self absorbed	Ambitious
Intrusive	Fragile	Arrogant
Shy	Tense	Grumpy
Altruistic	Polite	Sincere
Confident	Jealous	Cautious

Enthusiastic	Crafty	Sensitive
Boring	Harsh	Fair
Tolerant	Rough	Critical
Stable	Humble	Brave

Keep in mind that this list is about your *most typical* partner choices. Try to be as objective as possible, not focusing on what you think you like but what you actually end up with for the most part.

Attractive Traits List	Unattractive Traits List	Common List

Now, notice if the most common attributes match the list of people with anxious, avoidant or secure attachment style on pages 38 and 39. For example, as a general rule, people with anxious attachment are usually loving, loyal, dependable, generous, unpredictable, fragile... People with avoidant style are somehow self absorbed, cold, unavailable, practical, logical, independent... If you tend to date people with anxious style you are probably avoidant or secure/avoidant. If you tend to date people with avoidant style, you are probably anxious or secure/anxious. You can also pull your Imago Workup sheet again and see if you find any similarities between your partners' traits and your parents' profiles (add new ones if discovered or circle the ones that repeat on all lists). This is where it would be interesting to know your parent's attachment style, but we won't go into that - you may be able to guess it by now!

> *"One must learn to express his emotional experience, his anxieties as well as his needs, in an atmosphere of true sympathy, in order to find out that communication of emotional experience is not a danger but a relief..."*
>
> Edith Wieigert, The *Courage to Love*

PART FOUR: AWARENESS OF MY TRUE NEEDS

The fourth important part of this journey is to identify your emotional needs. Since our model of attachment influences how each of us reacts to our needs and how we go about getting them met, it is important that we become conscious of them. Being loved is a deep need. The deepest emotional needs are met through long-term, committed partnerships. When we fall in love, we open up our hearts to our partner, and this opens up some deep vulnerabilities. Literature and therapists emphasize how important it is to communicate "our needs" and how it is a trait of secure attachment. However, in my practice, I find this is one of the most difficult steps because most of us don't know what we need until we don't have it. Also, since being unaware of our needs is a trait of avoidant style attachment, people tend to think that they don't need much, as well as believing that it is good that they don't. Since understanding what you need at an emotional level, learning how to provide it for yourself, and asking your partner for it when appropriate, are all big elements of secure healthy relationships, we will spend some time on this topic.

According to Janae B. Weinhold Ph.D. & Barry K. Weinhold Ph.D. in their book *The Flight from Intimacy* (2008): "the sources of all major conflicts in relationships between adults can be found in their unmet developmental needs or unhealed developmental traumas." Shirley Jean Schmidt, MA, LPC author of the Developmental Needs Strategy Protocol –DNMS (2009), corroborates this statement. The DNMS, an ego state form of psychotherapy which treats attachment wounds, is based on the assumption that the degree to which developmental needs were not adequately met is the degree to which a client is stuck in childhood.

The Weinholds created the Developmental Systems Theory which suggests that relationships go through the same four developmental stages that individuals go through. If we get stuck or don't complete one or more of these stages we tend to have issues as adults while attempting to complete or resolve them (Weinhold & Weinhold, 2008).

The stages they propose are:

1. Co-dependency or bonding (conception to 6 months):

   The main needs at this stage are for loving and consistent care, hugging, nurturing touch, gaze, talk, many sensory experiences, uninterrupted expression, lots of conversation and eye contact in a comfortable and protective environment in order to meet the child's needs for safety and survival.

2. Counter-dependency or separation (6 to 36 months):

3. At this stage the child is able to complete psychological separation from her parents. She learns to safely explore her environment, internalizes appropriate physical and social limits, develops healthy narcissism, resolves conflict between oneness and separateness ("I am ok," "You are ok"), bonds with herself, has validating experiences, responds to child-initiated play, receives two yeses for every no, receives protection from harm, experiences celebration over her ability to think, reasons with information, has permission to express positive and negative feelings, and begins to identify self-needs as opposed to the needs of others.

4. Independence or mastery (3 to 6 years):

   A child continues to master self-care and becoming a functionally autonomous individual in this stage, separate from his parents. He starts developing his own core values and beliefs, and experiences bonding with nature and peers while developing empathy and respect for others. The child learns effective emotional self-regulation and appropriate deferred gratification of his own wants and needs while learning to trust his inner sense of wisdom and guidance.

5. Cooperation or interdependence (6 to 29 years):

Here the person learns to cooperate and negotiate with others. They acquire negotiation skills to get their needs met in healthy ways while trying to find solutions to conflicts that honor the needs of all parties involved. They are capable of experiencing secure bonding with peers, adults, nature, and culture while living authentically. They learn to accept responsibility for personal behaviors. Because the person can be strongly in-tune with self, others and the environment, they can continue to develop and nurture a sense of self while being able to reach out and connect with others. A person can both "go away" (be alone) and "come back" (be together).

While you, I, and others in our society are encouraged to develop independence and individuality, this doesn't mean that everyone will become a strong interdependent person. Only independent people can become interdependent, and only dependent people can become independent since we cannot skip stages. Depending on where the deficiency happened for us in these stages, we tend to gravitate towards an anxious or avoidant attachment style. The goal is to complete our developmental needs so that we can become interdependent and more fully developed.

Most people tend to get stuck in the first two stages because their need to experience consistent unconditional love and nurturing as well as their need for separation and individuation weren't mastered. People who experienced love and connection but on an inconsistent basis tend to develop anxious style attachment. People who experienced a lack of emotional engagement or too much independence too early tend to develop avoidant style attachment.

There are also people who experienced a lot of violence and anger, or had parents with severe cases of depression and addictions; they would learn what we call disorganized style: "I want to be close, but what if I get hurt?" (We call this the "love and hate" pattern.) If you don't seem to clearly fall into the anxious or avoidant style, you might fall into the disorganized category. You can find more information about the disorganized style here: http://www.psychalive.org/disorganized-attachment/.

If some or most of your traits are from the disorganized style, your need for safety wasn't satisfied in your early years and this will be the thing you will need the most (from yourself and from your partner when in a relationship). Regardless of your style, the healing steps are the same for all styles, with more focus on specific aspects for each one. In this guide we are focusing on anxious and avoidant styles primarily. To focus on the disorganized style, you would need to understand trauma and this requires more in depth and complex theory. If you suspect your style is disorganized, professional help is a must.

Our early developmental needs permeate our existence and manifest in our day to day lives. We all experience all of them since they are human needs, but sometimes we have learned to repress or even live without being in touch with many of them because those needs were never satisfied for us. We may have even been told that we shouldn't feel them, or we just needed to survive and make the best of our circumstances, so we adapted. Some of those needs are developmental requirements for us to become emotionally healthy.

Hopefully this section will help you learn more about the needs that were particularly overlooked for you, and you can start attending to them. Looking at your day to day triggers tends to be the best entry into those core underlying needs. When you feel triggered and experience an intense emotion, listen to it. Ask what would decrease that feeling in that moment even if you could never get it, it sounds ridiculous, or it seems like "too much" etc.

What follows are some tools that may be useful in putting words to those feelings or needs that can be hard for most of us to articulate. If we go back to the very beginning, Abraham Maslow (1943) was the first person to classify our needs:

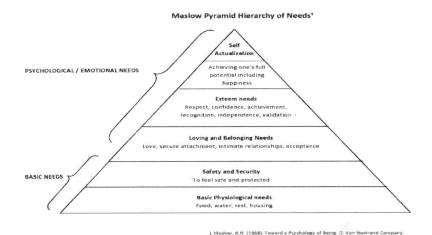

Sometimes people find it difficult to wrap their heads around abstract statements like these without any context, so I have developed some prompters to help you see if you are getting your needs met. There are two ways of filling out this exercise: 1) Read the sentences in the categories below and see which ones resonate with you without a particular reason. Mark these with an "x." Or 2) think of a painful event or situation that you are curious about and open to explore. As you read the lists, see which statements catch your attention the most and mark them with an "x." Those are likely the ones that carry the most information about what you needed or need that you didn't and still don't get. If you don't find an exact one, try choosing one that is the closest. Below the lists, I have provided some example ideas for you. These examples illustrate both ways of doing this exercise.

Basic Survival:

I will survive

My basic needs of food and others will be met

I deserve to live

My life is desired and important

Safety and Control:

I'll be safe

I can be in control sometimes

I can have choices sometimes

I am strong sometimes

I can get what I want sometimes without logical justifications

Security, Predictability and Stability:

Things will be okay!

I have a need for support. Can you be there for me?

Will you still be there even if I tell you this or you know me completely?

Love, Connection and Relationships:

I am lovable, loved, and loving

You will be there for me (I can count on people)

You go away and you come back

I am important to you and to people

I can be with you without losing myself or losing you

I can be taken care of sometimes

There will be space for my needs; they will be heard and can be satisfied a good number of times

<u>Acceptance and Belonging in Relationships:</u>

I fit somewhere

I am ok the way I am (looks, feelings, way of thinking, taste, preferences)

I am part of a family, group, community, culture

It is ok if I am different

It is ok to show my emotions

It is ok to share my needs (I won't be minimized, told they are wrong or that I shouldn't have them)

It is ok to let it out sometimes

I can be vulnerable

<u>Esteem and Identity:</u>

I know who I am

I am a good person

I am ok as I am. I know I am good enough!

I am worthy, I am worthwhile

I am deserving; I deserve (can have) good things

I am (can be) healthy

I am fine (attractive/lovable)

I am intelligent (able to learn)

I am significant (important)

I can trust myself and be trusted

Confidence and Self-Respect:

I am smart and capable enough

I can achieve and move along in life

I can be successful sometimes

I can trust my judgment

I can choose whom to trust

I can take care of myself

I deserve (can be) to be happy

I did/do the best I could and it is enough

I am respected by others

It is ok to make mistakes

Separation and Independence:

I need to be able to go away and come back

I need to be heard, express my opinions

I need to be me

I need mirroring/ being seen: I want you to see me and understand/get me

I need validation. I need to know that I am ok and my feelings are ok even when different from yours

Here are examples of a distressing situation and the corresponding need or feeling:

> *When my partner criticizes me, I need to know /feel that... I am ok as a person and that it is ok to make a mistake.*

> *When my partner doesn't call me, I need to know/feel that... He/she leaves but will come back and that I am loved.*

> *When my partner cries, I need to know/feel that... even though my actions hurt him/her I am still a good enough person.*

> *When I have a deadline, I need to know/feel that... things will be ok and that I can be in control sometimes.*

> *When I look for a job, I need to know/feel that...that I am intelligent and that things will be ok.*
>
> *When I enter a party, I need to know/feel that... I am attractive enough and that people will accept me.*
>
> *(your own)*

If you still have difficulty finding the answers, you may also start by getting in touch with what you *feel* first, which might directly guide you into what the *need* is. Here are examples using the immediate *feeling*, making it easier to identify the corresponding need in the situation:

> *When my partner criticizes me, I don't want to **feel like I am not good enough**. I need to know that...I am ok as a person and that it is ok to make a mistake.*
>
> *When my partner doesn't call me, I **feel scared and abandoned as if he/she doesn't care about me anymore**. I need to know that...He/she leaves but will come back and that I am loved.*
>
> *When my partner cries, I **feel as if I have done something wrong because I am bad**. I need to know that...even though my actions hurt him/her I am still a good enough person.*
>
> *When I have a deadline, I **feel out of control and panic**. I need to know that...things will be ok and that I can be in control sometimes.*

*When I look for a job, I **feel rejected and not worthy**. I need to know that...I am intelligent and that things will be ok.*

*When I enter a party, I **feel ugly and that everybody criticizes me**. I need to know that...I am attractive enough and that people will accept me.*

(your own)

PART FIVE: AWARENESS OF MY UNDERLYING CHILDHOOD ASSUMPTIONS

Connecting more deeply with your true needs will also help you to uncover very important underlying assumptions that fuel unhealthy attachment reactions. We will do this using the following list inspired by the Attachment Needs Ladder from Shirley Jean Schmidt's Development Needs Meeting Strategy model (2009). Usually with long term deprivation or inconsistent care, we end up developing correlating underlying thoughts or cognitions about ourselves that make sense to us at the time but that aren't true. Under unfortunate circumstances and imperfect life situations, we internalize them, adapt, and come up with negative assumptions about ourselves in order to make sense of what is going on.

Below is a list of negative beliefs wounded children might acquire in childhood when attachment needs aren't adequately met. The list divides our unconscious needs into four categories. When you are ready, focus your attention on a disturbing current or childhood event. As you focus on the event, scan the list of negative beliefs and observe which statements resonate with you the most in relation to that event. Try not to think too hard; just let your unconscious feel whatever it feels. Don't question or judge why you would think that way. Remember that the negative belief may exist at a very subtle or deep level; questioning might take you away from the experience.

When I think of (event/situation)...

I feel like...

My Existence...

I shouldn't be here

My life doesn't matter

I don't deserve to be alive

I am so alone; there is no point to my life

My life isn't acceptable

My Physical and Sexual Safety...

The world isn't safe enough

I am very vulnerable, I feel in constant danger

I am scared most of the time

I don't deserve to be safe

It is not possible to be safe

Everyone is there to hurt/get me

I can't trust anyone

I must hide or disappear or be invisible to be safe

I must be a people pleaser or peacemaker to stay safe

I must keep my guard up most of the time to be safe

My Emotional Safety...

There is no safe place for me

I feel very vulnerable and fragile most of the time

Most people seem dangerous

Everybody can or would hurt me

It is difficult for me to trust people

It is difficult for me to feel safe being myself or showing who I am

Nobody cares about my needs

Nobody cares about my feelings

It is better to hide or disappear or be invisible to be ok

I must be a people pleaser or peacemaker to be ok

I must keep my guard up most of the time to be ok

My Sense of Self and My Personal Identity...

I don't know who I am

I don't deserve to have a self

It is bad to want a self

I must not been seen or heard

I must not grow

I must not individuate

I must not have needs

I don't matter

Others tell me who I am, what I feel, what I like, what I believe

I can be an object, but not a person

I must let others smother or engulf me

I must not set or maintain interpersonal boundaries

I must do for others, even when it is not good for me

My Relationship to Others...

I depend on others to feel secure

I need lots of attention from others to feel secure

I must be very emotionally close to others to feel secure

I cannot tolerate being alone

I cannot tolerate rejection

I cannot tolerate people leaving me

I cannot tolerate criticism

Others must comfort me when I am upset or insecure because I can't do it for myself

Others must meet my emotional needs because I can't do it myself

I am and always will be completely alone

People will accept me if I don't have needs

People will reject me if I have needs

People will inevitably ignore me

People will inevitably disappoint me

People will inevitably abandon me

I must rely solely on myself

I cannot depend on others

I must not get emotionally close to others

I must not let others get emotionally close to me

I must not ask for comfort, advice, or help

I must not share my private thoughts or feelings

I must not share with others how I truly feel deep down inside

I must comfort myself when I am upset, because others cannot/will not

I must meet my own emotional needs, because others cannot/will not

To conclude both sections on needs and assumptions, I want to share some thoughts from *"The Flight from Intimacy"* book. Dr. Weinhold summarizes which reactions we should have experienced from our primary caregivers in order not to have developed unhealthy wounds. It is helpful to reflect on them since these kinds of reactions are what we need to practice towards ourselves, our partner and children in the present. Of course, no human can do this perfectly all the time, but practice them as much as possible as you work towards a more secure attachment. Take some time to reflect on the ways you didn't get these interactions below. Consider how you can now practice healthy interactions with yourself or ask for them in current relationships. Just observe your answers for now as we will expand on the action topic in Chapter Four.

What I needed from my parents when I was young:

- To have reacted calmly and reassuringly to any of my aggressive impulses
- To have supported my attempts to become separate and autonomous instead of being threatened by them
- To have allowed me to experience and express my natural feelings and urges such as rage, fear, jealousy, and defiance
- To have allowed me to develop and follow my natural curiosity safely during each developmental stage, rather than

overprotecting me or requiring me to do things to please them
- To have been available both physically and emotionally when I needed them
- To have permitted me to express conflicting or ambivalent feelings and treat those feelings seriously and with respect
- To have seen me as separate from them, as someone with my own needs, wishes, fears, dreams, and accomplishments (Weinhold, et al., 2008).

PART SIX: AWARENESS OF THE ROOTS OF MY FRUSTRATIONS

"Behind each anger is a hurt, and behind each hurt is an unmet longing or need." *Imago Relationships International*

In this section we will try to connect the current feelings we are experiencing to their origin in the past. In this way, we can separate it from the present and understand how all of the emotional charge doesn't belong only to the present situation. After gaining awareness of your deepest needs and underlying assumptions, now is a good time to complete the earlier exercise about your frustrations from page 42. The fourth and fifth parts of the exercise involve completing the sections about your underlying fears and identifying what you need by connecting those feelings and deficiencies to specific events in your past.

Since we are talking about developmental processes, for some people it might be difficult or impossible to retrieve specific moments. That is ok and normal. So just try to find out if you felt that way (the underlying fear and unmet need identified) for long periods of time in your life or for most of your life and go with that. Another tip that might help you to get in touch with those feelings is to review the positive and negative traits from your care takers from page 41 and picture yourself as a little child in front of that person while he/she was... (insert positive or negative trait). For example: "When my dad was aloof...I felt empty or lost." The purpose of this awareness is to increase empathy and understanding of the feelings and therefore motivate yourself or your partner to meet the need so that you can start healing from your past.

For each frustrating situation you documented on page 43, you can now add:

4- My Underlying Fear is...

> Ex: *feeling invisible, ignored, devalued, disapproved, dominated, shamed, neglected...*
>
> And the story that I tell myself (assumptions) is...
>
> Ex: *That I don't matter, that my opinions aren't important*
>
> Based on the following past childhood memory(ies) (if identified)...

Ex: *when not being included in the adult conversations during meals*

5- What I really need is...

Ex: *to remind myself that I matter even when people or my partner don't respond to me for whatever reason (individual work)*

Note: if you can't think that you matter at all, more individual therapy would be recommended.

Ex: *Behavioral change request from partner: Responses- I need you to try to respond to my conversations so I can feel seen and that my presence matters (relational work)*

The following is an example of this complete exercise:

1. Typical Behavior:

    Ex: When you don't answer my questions...

2. Typical Feelings...

    Ex: Angry, sad, lonely, alienated, withdrawn, disappointed, rejected, trapped, irritated

3. My Typical Reaction:

    Ex: Screaming, shutting down, nagging, withdrawing, pulling away ...

4- My Underlying Fear is...

Ex: feeling invisible, ignored, devalued, disapproved, dominated, guilty, shamed, neglected...

And the story that I tell myself (assumptions) is...

Ex: That I don't matter, that my opinions aren't important

Based on the following past childhood memory(ies) (if identified)...

Ex: when not being included in the adult conversations during meals

5- What I really need from now on is...

Ex: to remind myself that I matter even when people or my partner don't respond to me for whatever reason (individual work)

Ex: Behavioral change request from partner: Responses- I need you to try to respond to my conversations so I can feel seen and that my presence matters (relational work)

It is important to note that a partner needs to be genuinely willing and able to accept and commit to this kind of work. If it doesn't feel right or possible, other options should be explored that will work for both people while each person does more individual work. Any blocks that happen in responding to your partner's needs (or vice versa) are directly pointing to individual areas of growth.

PART SEVEN: AWARENESS OF HOW I FEEL MOST TAKEN CARE OF

The next area for you to gain awareness in is identifying the main interactions or gestures that make you feel secure, loved, close, and connected in a relationship. According to the author of the popular book "Five Love Languages," Dr. Gary D. Chapman (2015), most people have different preferences when it comes to how love is communicated to them. We come from different attachment styles which causes us to have different love languages. In general, the five love languages are: words of affirmation, acts of service, affection, quality time, and gifts. Of course, each category requires more in depth exploration since each definition is very personal. Take some time to explore what each one means to you. The more specific the better! To find out which love language is strongest for you, visit http://www.5lovelanguages.com/ and take the test.

You will find that some or most of them have a lot in common with your emotional needs. Once you identify the basic underlying need, you can find the best way (in this case the language category) that satisfies it. This will give you some specific ways to satisfy those needs.

When you really want to show someone you care about them, which way comes to your mind first? Your most basic instincts can show your primary love language as well. This would relate to your needs. Remember that what is best for you might not necessarily be best for your partner or for others. In order to achieve a secure attachment style, we need to have our needs met and meet our partner's needs frequently and consistently enough. There is no magic number, but our needs should be met more often than not.

After you have compiled a few or many of your insights, you can record them on the list provided below. Call this list "Caring Behaviors" (www.pairs.org) for both you and your significant other to remember to attend to. You can provide more than one option of ways in which your needs can be fulfilled. Making the requests clear, concrete and specific in both content and time would be extremely helpful (some examples are provided below). If you are in a relationship, remember to keep an eye on your partner's list too. At first, you will have a tendency to forget all of them (which is why they became deficiencies in the first place!) Now you have an opportunity to re-parent yourself. Ask your partner for help, and help your partner so that both of you can achieve a more secure attachment style and enjoy your relationship better. This is a perfect example of how a combination of intrapersonal/individual and relational work can help us find healing.

If you are single, you can find ways to provide this for yourself. We will learn more about this in the section about Inner Child work.

Insert the word "My" or "My partner's" before Caring Behaviors and print as many copies as you need. A few examples are listed to get you started and an empty sheet follows for you to print or make as many copies as you need.

Caring Behaviors							
Example of Caring behaviors	Mon	Tues	Wed	Thurs	Fri	Sat	Sun
1- Looking deeply into my eyes at least once a week							
2- Initiating talks about how to improve the relationship and other spiritual matters every other week							
3-Asking me about my work and							

hobbies weekly							
4- Showing me affection (hugs, kisses, nice gestures) anytime with no reason every other day							
5- Surprising me with by suggesting something I want to do : shopping, watching a particular movie, going to a concert/game …once a month							

6- Cooking for me my favorite meal (chili) once every other week.							
7- Making an effort to give me 30 minutes by myself when we get home every day.							
8- Suggesting that I go out with my friends once a month.							
9- Running an errand for me once a week							

10-Making the effort to stay in touch with my parents once a month							

(Adjusted from Pairs Mastery Program Handbook, 1999)

For your personal use:

Caring Behaviors	Mon	Tues	Wed	Thurs	Fri	Sat	Sun

PART EIGHT: AWARENESS OF HIDDEN AGENDAS AND EXPECTATIONS

The final area for us to cover is the area of hidden agendas and expectations. Since we are social creatures our environments, families and society play a huge role in what our world is. As Weinhold, PhD. suggests, families, countries and societies tend to reinforce certain values that encourage a certain attachment style. In my experience with Latin culture, they tend to be more prompt to enmeshment. Codependency values are reinforced, and I see more trouble in achieving separation and differentiation. In the Western society the value of independence is highly respected and reinforced, therefore, more messages that support an avoidant style tend to be embraced.

Hidden expectations are a very important aspect to figure out because as the word states, they are hidden. Looking into and answering some of the following questions will bring you some insight into hidden agendas that we all carry but don't know until we start having trouble:

  a. How was your parents' relationship? How did they show love to each other and show you love growing up? What made you feel the most loved as a child?
  b. Did your parents fight? If so, who would win? Did you see them apologize to each other and/or achieve reconciliation or not?
  c. What are the gender roles you do or do not subscribe to? Typical traditional or more egalitarian? In either case, which areas do they involve? House chores, financial

responsibilities, child care, leisure decisions, communication style (use of more open ended questions vs. ordering and frequency)?
d. What did you learn in society about your role as a man/woman, boyfriend / girlfriend, husband/wife? How does that influence your expectations from your partner?
e. What messages do you follow in regards to the concepts of dependency and independency, being alone or with someone, age differences, and family pressures regarding marriage, singlehood or divorce?

It is a good time for a break since we will now be switching gears and getting into new territory. Good job! After gaining all this insight, you are probably pretty sure of your predominant attachment style. But insight isn't enough. So get ready for some action steps towards gaining a more secure attachment style!

CHAPTER FOUR

Healthy Attachment and Retraining Your Brain

"To persevere with the will to understand in the face of obstacles is the heroism of consciousness." Nathaniel Branden, *The Six Pillars of Self-Esteem*

The final and most challenging phase of healing your attachment style is to use all this information to train your brain differently. As Lisa Firestone, PhD (2013) states, our attachment style is driven mostly by the limbic part of our brain and shapes our daily interactions. Individual differences in attachment style have an impact on affect regulation, information processing, and communication in close relationships because our internal working models shape our cognitive, emotional, and behavioral responses to others (Cassidy & Shaver, et al., 2008). Instead of letting your brain be in charge, you can take the driver's seat and start observing and changing the way your brain (your attachment style) responds.

The best way to start is to carry all of your new found awareness to a current situation, slow down, and figure out how it applies to you. How can you now act differently? The next four steps will describe how we can:

1. Embrace, validate and soothe our feelings

2. Identify, challenge and rewrite cognitive distortions

3. Identify new actions and possibilities based on healthy behaviors and secure relational attachment

4. Maintain healthy behaviors while identifying ongoing obstacles

STEP ONE: EMBRACING MY FEELINGS

In Part One of Chapter Three we began to explore feelings with the purpose of gaining a greater awareness of how they help to indicate your attachment style. Emotions are the main ingredient in relationships. We wouldn't be in relationships if we didn't have emotions. In order to improve your relationship EQ, you need to be open to explore and better handle your emotions. What are the feelings that you experience the most and in what situations? Knowing your triggers is the first step to start doing something about it. To begin this step, I would like to introduce you to a very important aspect of psychology called "Acceptable Window of Tolerance."

> *"Only when we truly accept ourselves, we change."*
>
> Carl Rogers, father of Client-Centered Therapy, most influential American psychologist of the 20th century

When we talk about feelings or emotions, the first thing that often comes to mind is somebody out of control who needs to be calmed down. Do you agree? This can be true; emotions can get out of control and soothing and regulating them is necessary. However, people with avoidant attachment style tend to lack consistent emotional presence, so I would like to focus more deeply on this very important aspect. The goal is to be within the ideal "window of tolerance" as much as possible so that we can best manage life and relationships. Naturally, people with a secure attachment style are able to do this best.

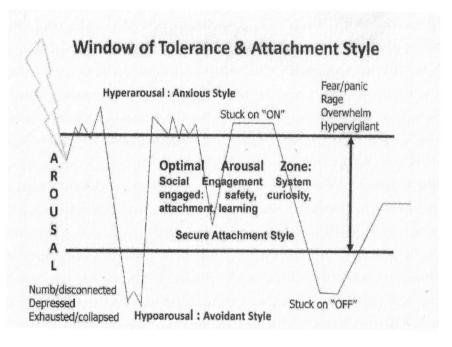

©Levine, 1997; Siegel, 1999; Ogden and Minton, 2000; Porges, 2005

As you have probably observed, there are four scenarios when it comes to emotional tolerance: people who are above the horizontal top line (generally, people with anxious attachment who have difficulty regulating emotions), people below the bottom horizontal line (generally, people with avoidant attachment style who have more difficulty staying connected and emotionally present), people with disorganized style who tend to move from one extreme to the other, and people with secure attachment style who are able to stay within the window of tolerance when under stress.

The following is a preparation exercise that is actually useful for all styles since it is simply about tuning in and embracing your feelings. If you are avoidant it might take some time to get in touch with your feelings or even identify them since you tend to repress them. This doesn't mean they are not there! Daily practice will help you start to get in touch with them. If you are anxious, you may have no trouble experiencing your feelings but probably struggle with regulating them or clearly identifying them because they are too intense or you experience so many at one time.

Here is the exercise: three times a day, check in and see how you are feeling. You could do this for a general situation that has just happened or for anything else that comes up in the moment. Record the feeling, its intensity and where you feel it in your body. Then continue on with your life. It takes a few minutes, but it is a good first step to reconnect and learn about ourselves. Most people have difficulty identifying their feelings and finding words to express them clearly. Looking at this list might help you put your feelings into words more easily. Carry this sheet with you so you can use it when unpredictable situations come up.

Emotional Vocabulary List

The main problem when talking about feelings is that most people don't have the vocabulary to express them. This is a problem, because descriptive words help us understand ourselves and the world around us. If we don't have enough names for our emotions, it's hard to get a handle on what we're feeling when an emotion arises. According to experts, having a larger and more precise vocabulary makes us more articulate, more able to express nuance and subtlety and helps us identify things more quickly. This can be very helpful when emotions are concerned! The sooner you know what you're feeling, the quicker you can take effective emotional action:

Aggressive	Exhausted	Open
Aggravated	Fearful	Pained
Alienated	Fulfilled	Panicked
Angry	Frightened	Paranoid
Annoyed	Frustrated	Peaceful
Anxious	Guilty	Pessimistic
Apathetic	Happy	Playful
Arrogant	Helpless	Pleased
Bashful	Helpful	Proud
Bored	Hopeful	Puzzled

Cautious	Hostile	Regretful
Confident	Humiliated	Relieved
Confused	Hurt	Resentful
Content	Hysterical	Sad
Curious	Innocent	Satisfied
Critical	Indifferent	Shocked
Depressed	Indecisive	Shy
Determined	Impatient	Sorry
Detached	Interested	Stubborn
Disappointed	Intuitive	Sure
Discouraged	Insecure	Surprised
Disconnected	Jealous	Suspicious
Disgusted	Lonely	Thoughtful
Embarrassed	Loved	Trustful
Enthusiastic	Lovestruck	Undecided
Envious	Mischievous	Withdrawn
Ecstatic	Miserable	Worried
Excited	Negative	

	Optimistic	

Keep in mind that there are some feelings each style tends to more prominently experience. So see if you find this list helpful as well:

Anxious Style Typical Feelings	Avoidant Style Typical Feelings
Abandoned	Shut down
Sad/Depressed	Indifferent
Unappreciated	Distrustful
Resentful	Hateful
Angry	Resentful
Scared	Overwhelmed
Unsettled	Out of control
Rejected	Engulfed
Despaired	In trouble
Hopeless	Empty
Lonely	Restless
Irritated	Alone
Jealous	Misunderstood
Guilty	Frustrated
Defeated	Angry
Overwhelmed	Deceived
Hateful	
Unlovable	Aloof
Negative / Pessimistic	

In loved quickly and intensely Out of control Loving Better than/Defective	Better than

Life is feeling. To not feel is to be dead. To be at peace with all feelings and to learn to deal with them without being overwhelmed or disconnected from them is a sign of secure attachment. According to Nobel peace prize winner, exiled Vietnamese monk Thich Nhat Hanh, there are three types of feelings: pleasant, unpleasant, and neutral. We will now look at three ways to deal with all of your feelings which will help you gear yourself towards a more secure attachment.

VALIDATING AND SOOTHING OUR FEELINGS

What can we do when we experience certain uncomfortable feelings? First of all, be compassionate towards yourself. Your intrinsic reactions (thoughts, feelings) will probably stay the same for awhile, so try to be accepting and patient with yourself. Also, understanding your history (this is what we explored in Chapter Three) will help you start to understand that your feelings and reactions make sense and that they are a result of a combination of aspects. Most people say that feelings don't make sense, but in my experience once you take the time to listen to people's histories, they make a lot of sense. Be open to that possibility. As you tune in to your feelings, try not to run away from them. Feelings are our most primitive source of information, so if we listen we can learn a lot about our needs and therefore satisfy them. If we stay present, validate and soothe feelings, we can decrease their intensity, get this information, and move on.

The main medicine for feelings is VALIDATION. The more you validate them the more they dissipate. Emotional validation is the process of learning about, understanding, and expressing acceptance of another person's emotional experience. (Feil, The Validation Breakthrough, 2012)

To validate someone's feelings is to first be open and curious about someone's feelings. Next, it is to understand them, and finally it is to nurture them. When we validate someone, we allow them to safely share their feelings and thoughts. We are reassuring them that it is okay to have the feelings they have. We are demonstrating that we will still accept them after they have shared their feelings. We help them feel heard, acknowledged, understood and accepted. And all of this can and should be applied to our own selves.

Validation comes naturally to people with secure attachment style and is a big deficiency in people with other attachments types. It is not a coincidence that people with secure attachment are more resilient. The next time you compare yourself to somebody who seems to bounce back from a difficult situation quickly, don't think it is because they are stronger than you and you are weak. They are probably lucky to have a secure attachment style.

How does this happen? The view of adult attachment theory is one of the latest measures used to determine the level of psychological distress people experience during stressful circumstances. Research shows how secure attachment serves as an inner resource in times of stress and how insecure attachment can be a risk factor that increases vulnerability and distress. Data has been found which reflects the ways adult attachment styles affect one's coping and emotional reactions when faced with the terror of personal death, military and war-related stressors, interpersonal losses, personal failure, parenthood related stressors, and chronic pain. (Shaver, & Mikulincer, 2012)

The basic premise is that secure attachment is an inner resource that helps a person to positively appraise stressful experiences, to constructively cope with these events, and to improve his or her well being and adjustment. As you probably understand by now, insecure attachment style (anxious or avoidant) can be viewed as a potential risk factor, leading to poor coping and maladjustment. Attachment theory is one of the most helpful psychological frameworks to understand and measure human reactions to two major life stressors: loss and separation.

Securely attached people tend to have optimistic expectations, view stressful events as painful but manageable, have higher levels of self efficacy and look for help when needed. People with insecure attachment styles present higher level of distress, unstable and inadequate affect regulation methods and a low sense of personal efficacy. Separation isn't viewed as a resolvable episode. It triggers all the fears of abandonment that impede healthy functioning and the embracing of daily life. (Mikulincer, Florian, & Tolmacz, 1990)

For people with insecure attachment to gain a more secure style, validation is a powerful tool to start using today. For anxious people, it is very helpful because it calms them very quickly allowing them to access more of their neurocortex and logical functions. For avoidant people, it helps them to get in touch with hidden emotions. Instead of resorting too much or too quickly to their logic they can become aware and connect with their feelings and then with other people.

Here are some simple ways to validate yourself or someone else (Feil, et al., 2012):

Awww

Yeah

Mmm

I hear you

That hurts

That's not good

That's no fun

Wow, that's a lot to deal with

I would feel the same way

I'd feel sad/hurt/angry/jealous, etc. too

That is sad

That sounds discouraging

That sounds like it would really hurt

That must really hurt

I know just what you mean

I would feel the same way

I can understand how you feel

It sounds like you are really feeling _____

It sounds like _____ is really important to you

For some people all you need to do is use these short, validating comments and they will continue to talk. For others, you might encourage them to keep talking with short questions such as:

Really?

Yeah?

How's that?

You did?

She did?

If you find yourself in a position of needing to lead the conversation you might try:

I can see that you are really upset

You look pretty sad

You seem a little worried, troubled, scared, etc.

Would you like to talk about it?

That really bothered you, didn't it?

How did you feel when _____?

Also, to help someone release their feelings try:

What bothers you the most about it?

How strongly are you feeling that (on a scale of 0-10)?

How come? How so? How's that?

So you really felt _____? Is that close?

So what bothered you was that _____?

What else bothered you?

How else did you feel?

What would help you feel better?

Often, the fewer words from you, the better, especially when someone needs to talk and they are both willing and able. I have found, as I am sure you have, that it takes more to get some people talking than others. But once most people start and feel safe and validated, they will continue.

Because we already know that attachment and general security are associated with many positive personal and social outcomes, and validation is one of the ways to achieve it, start practicing it today towards yourself and the people around you. It will help to increase people's sense of security on a lasting basis.

By validating, we are naming the emotions which engage the limbic system (right brain) and help to calm it down. We then become more open for logical information and solutions (left brain). In this way, we promote a more integrated mind and better emotional health.

Neuropsychiatrist and pioneer in the field of interpersonal neurobiology Dan J. Siegel (2012) discuss this technique in his book the *Whole Brain Child*: NAME IT TO TAME IT. "Corral raging right-brain behavior through left-brain storytelling, appealing to the left brain's affinity for words and reasoning to calm emotional storms and bodily tension." When a person has an integrated and balanced brain, what Siegel calls "a whole brain", s/he has access to both sides when needed in an appropriate way. For example, when it is time to feel sadness because of a death or something upsetting, the person feels it, uses his/her left brain to put feelings into words and help soothe those feelings.

With mindfulness we will be doing some of the work necessary for this to happen. By naming the feelings, we are helping them calm down so we can then access the left part of our brain to help with their processing and healthy resolution. In this way we can move into solutions or logical thinking when and if it is appropriate to the situation.

MINDFUL OBSERVANCE

Mindfulness can be described as "a deliberate, nonjudgmental attention to experience in the present moment." Siegel, 2007, Kabat-Zinn, 2005 & Wallin, 2007 (as cited in Lumiere, 2012). The purpose of both validation and mindfulness practice is to provide an internalized secure base. Attunement, whether it is internal in mindfulness or interpersonal in attachment, is what leads to a sense of this secure base (Siegel, 2010).

> "While mindfulness is not part of the vocabulary of attachment, this construct from Buddhist Psychology seems a natural outgrowth of attachment theory and research. . . The regular exercise of mindful awareness seems to promote the same benefits - bodily and affective self-regulation, attuned communication with others, insight, empathy, and resilience - that research has found to be associated with childhood histories of secure attachment. . . Although there might be other explanations for these parallel outcomes, I would suggest that they arise from the fact that mindfulness and secure attachment alike are capable of generating—though by very different routes—the same invaluable psychological resource, namely an internalized secure base." Siegel & Wallin, 2007, p. 5-6 (as cited in Lumiere, 2012)

At the heart of this process is a form of internal "tuning in" to oneself which enables people to become their own best caretaker. Just as our attunement to our children promotes a healthy, secure attachment, tuning in to our self also promotes a foundation for more secure attachment. It is important to have a direct experience of loving attunement within. (Siegel, et. al, 2010) This inner attunement can be provided through any mindfulness practice.

When we have an unpleasant feeling we tend to want to chase it away. However, we need to remember that it is a feeling and it shall pass. We need to return to our conscious breathing because by calming our bodies (which actually calms the amygdala in our brains, the part that is detecting some danger and is ready to go into fight, flight or freeze response as it is designed to do) we can regain a more balanced perspective on things. Tip: When breathing - try taking longer counts when exhaling than inhaling because that is the part that activates the parasympathetic nervous systems which calms us down. By naming the feeling and also locating it in our bodies (if possible), we can focus more on it and help it dissipate. With feelings it is contrary to what most people think- the more you stay with them and validate them, the more they dissipate and go away. If we dismiss them, minimize or ignore them the more intense they become.

Calling a feeling by its name, such as "anger," "sorrow," "happiness," " frustration," "joy," "envy" etc, helps us clearly identify them and recognize them more deeply. We try to be neither drowned nor terrorized by the feelings, nor do we reject them. Our attitude of not clinging to or rejecting our feelings is the attitude of letting go, an important part of acceptance.

If we embrace our unpleasant feelings with an open heart, non judgmental attitude and compassion, we can transform them into the kind of energy that is healthy and has the capacity to nourish us. Through the work of mindful observation our unpleasant feelings can illuminate a lot for us, offering us insight into ourselves and the world. Think of your feelings as the panel or dashboard on a car. Every time a light goes on it is giving you information about something in or outside your car. This is the same role feelings play for us. This is why people who live in their left brain too much can miss important information about social cues and relationships. It can also be dangerous for survival. Most dangerous situations are perceived by our reptile or animal brain even though we might not have any evidence or logical information yet.

On the other hand, people who live too much in their right brain tend to be easily overwhelmed and out of control, and they lose perspective on practical solutions and objective information. The healthy answer is found in having the right balance of "middle ground" between our left and right brain, as with anything else in life. However, as you learn more about attachment styles, you may realize that your style tends to incline you more to one side than the other. Therefore, your task will be to practice the one that you have more of a deficiency with so you can develop a more whole brain balance between feelings/emotions and logic/solutions.

I want to encourage you again at this point to observe and accept feelings without judgment. Most people have learned that feelings are good or bad. Or even worse, that if you feel this or that you are "a good person" or "a bad person." That is so unhealthy because every human being will experience all type of feelings, from love to hate and everything in between, and this doesn't make you a better or worse person. Reflect on your mistaken beliefs about feelings in general or your own by being attuned to your reaction(s) when you feel something. How do you feel towards that? What is your secondary emotion? Do you judge yourself? Do you feel good about yourself? Do you sometimes feel good and bad at the same time? If your answer is yes, you have some work to do because feelings are just feelings. If you tend to judge yourself you may eventually suffer from low self esteem, self rejection and even depression. Start today by catching yourself every time you feel judgment and try to accept a neutral attitude. Keep track of certain feelings you can't change your attitude towards and if the inner judge impedes you from moving on with this work, you might benefit from some therapy. Accept that life is made of positive and negative emotions that won't last forever. If you are a person who wishes you could feel good all the time, you are not alone. But that isn't realistic or possible. Accept those negative times along with the good and positive, because you can't have one without the other. Just as there is night and day, there is sadness and happiness.

Most importantly, don't be afraid of your emotions. They are part of you and your identity and they help you be alive. Embrace them and learn to love yourself with everything that you are and feel. Don't judge yourself about what you feel since you can't control it and it isn't anybody's "fault." A lot of feelings are influenced by temperament and that is something we are born with. Just as some people are more sensitive to the sun or certain foods, some people are more emotionally sensitive and therefore feel more strongly or experience more of certain feelings. If this resonates with you, you are not alone. And fortunately Dr. Elaine Aron, MA, PhD. has dedicated her life to studying these traits because she herself is a highly sensitive person. She has a website full of information and resources if you would like to know more about it and learn to love the benefits of being such a type of person: http://www.hsperson.com/.

Whether you are a highly sensitive person or not, judgment or the belief that something is wrong with you is not only unhelpful, it is unfair to yourself and to others. Would you attack or look down on somebody for wearing sunscreen or for not eating peanuts? I think you get my point.

One of the most common ways to practice mindfulness is following guided meditations. In a little while, I will share a couple of them with you which my clients find particularly helpful when beginning this work. If you find yourself more open to the meditation practice, you can Google meditations online and find many options. If you don't think it is your thing or find yourself resistant to the language of other common meditations, these basic ones would be easier for you.

Getting Your Feet Wet in Mindfulness: a Word about Meditation and a Taste of It

The main ways to earn secure attachment are through meditation and psychotherapy. Tons of research is being conducted to prove exactly how this happens and how meditation works in the brain. So far, the general understanding is that by developing the relationship or connection between the adult and child ego states we create neuropathways that resemble the ones created from secure attachment. There is a lot more to be studied, but we will leave that to the researchers.

What matters for us here is that meditation works. One of the main things we have discovered so far is that our brain processes more thoughts and feelings during meditation than when you are simply relaxing. Is any kind of meditation ok? No. Choosing the right type is important, even more so when we are talking of trauma processing, attachment repairing and Inner Child work. Why? Because we need to create the compassionate and holding environment that we missed in childhood, and some types of meditation don't necessarily facilitate that.

A team of researchers at the Norwegian University of Science and Technology (NTNU), the University of Oslo and the University of Sydney sustain that different meditation techniques can actually be divided into two main groups. One type is concentrative meditation, where the meditating person focuses attention on his or her breathing or on specific thoughts and in doing so, suppresses other thoughts. The other type may be called nondirective meditation, where the person who is meditating effortlessly focuses on his or her breathing or on a meditation sound, but beyond that the mind is allowed to wander as it pleases. Some modern meditation methods are of this nondirective kind.

"The study indicates that nondirective meditation allows for more room to process memories and emotions than during concentrated meditation," says Svend Davanger, a neuroscientist at the University of Oslo, and co-author of the study. That is exactly what we are looking for: more processing of memories to encourage better affect regulation and more secure attachment. If you are like me, you might want to understand why this is. If you don't need to know the details or don't care, skip to the meditation section already and start getting your hands dirty!

Processing our memories is where the key is. Why? Because human nature is naturally geared towards health and being in meaningful relations with others. When life conditions are good, we thrive; when we're under prolonged periods of stress or disturbing events happen, symptoms can develop. Under high levels of stress the brain cannot process information normally and therefore, those experiences tend to get stuck in isolated neuropathways. Those moments become "frozen in time;" remembering a trauma may feel as bad as going through it the first time because the images, sounds, smells, and feelings haven't changed no matter how much time passes. Such unprocessed memories have a lasting negative effect that interferes with the way a person sees the world and relates to other people. (Shapiro, EMDR, 1990) Any way we can help the brain to naturally process those memories will be beneficial for our mental health.

Open/Explorative Meditations: First Exercise

So let's start practicing some. Please relax since this is not even close to anything you have heard of in the traditional meditations. Trust me. Be open and see what happens. You might be amazed. The way to start is simple. Sit up straight on a folded blanket or comfortable pillow. Use a chair if you prefer, or even lay on the floor if you think you can stay awake.

You've likely often heard to focus on the in and out breath. Try doing it. Don't try to manipulate the breath or do it in any special way other than breathing into the abdomen. Otherwise, just follow it. Do this alone for a few minutes and try noticing thoughts come and go. If a thought starts to take hold, listen to it, don't try to push it away and welcome it without self-judgment if possible. If you notice a judgment, then welcome it and do the same thing. Welcome it and pay attention to it for as long needed while continuing to breathe. You might learn a lot about yourself by just listening to what that judgment is about. Ask it about itself as if you were meeting a new person. Notice your body's sensations. Feel where the tension is bound up. Try releasing it progressively; using the breath as a center point and rhythm for the release if that is helpful. If nothing happens, that is ok. It just means those body tensions are there for a reason. Try focusing and being with them for as long as you can and see what happens. Continue to breathe. And that is it! There are no main goals of relaxation, clearing your mind, or anything. For some people the experience of doing something with no strings to a specific outcome attached is a new and healing experience in and of itself.

Open/Explorative Meditations: Second Exercise

A second exercise along the same lines is adapted from Internal Family Systems Model (IFS) and is called "Parts Meditation." (Credit to Institute for Self-Leadership. www.selfleadership.org)

Begin by taking some nice deep breaths for a little while

Notice your body in the chair

As you breathe deeply, scan your body for what we call "trailheads" (these could be points of pressure, congestion, stiffness, pain – anything in or around your body that doesn't feel like *you* exactly)

Scan your mind as well... Places of agitation in your mind... Places of dullness or fogginess...Anything that doesn't feel quite like *you*

As you do that scan, settle on one of those "trailheads" and then go ahead and just begin to gently focus on it, that place in your body or your mind, while you continue to breathe deeply

Gently focus on it, notice it, bring your awareness to it... And if you can, help it to notice you

Help it to notice that it's not alone... Let it know that you are there too...

If it's possible (and don't force anything) extend a kind of loving energy to that place in your body or your mind

At this point there might be something it wants you to know, which is fine

But the main point of this meditation is to help that part of you that is manifesting this way to know that it's not alone, that you are there with it

You can do that by, again, extending a loving energy to it, perhaps some loving words

Try one or all of these with a place in your body or mind. The purpose of the meditation right now is to help these parts know that they are not alone, that they are loved and they can relax because they are not alone... you are there too and they can begin to trust that

With some of them, as you extend the loving energy or comforting words or breath, you'll sense an immediate relaxing. There will be a shift in your body or your mind

But others won't shift, which is fine. It just means they need more attention before they can relax

They may need for you to hear more about them at some point... for them to feel more known by you

If you stay with one trailhead and it doesn't relax, you can make an appointment with it to talk with it later, and then move on to another

When you get to another trailhead, a point in your body or mind, extend a loving energy or comforting words into it...until you sense a shift

When a part does relax, you will notice a little more space in your body or mind... a little more openness

As you sense the spaciousness, it's possible to focus on that, that space inside

Notice what that's like

What you'll find is that it becomes a virtual cycle. The more space you feel, the more loving energy you bring to the parts

The more they trust you... the more they relax and the space there is for you

Feel the point where you feel increasingly IN your body ("embodied")... it's the parts and their burdens that keep you a little out of your body

If your parts have relaxed, notice what it's like to be in your body more

This becomes a kind of cycle also, where you become embodied and you bring that awareness to your parts

And they relax more and allow you to be in your body more

It's useful to be more and more familiar with this state of embodiment

So you can tell day to day, hour to hour, minute to minute how much you are and how much you are not in your body

When you sense that you are not, just go to the parts that are taking up space and help them relax, in just this way

This becomes a kind of practice and with practice you will find you can spend more and more time in your body, even when you aren't meditating like this

Even when you are in the world interacting with people...

When the time feels right, begin to shift your focus from this inside space in the body or the mind... shift it to the outside, first gently opening your eyes

Notice it's possible to stay in your body even while opening your eyes

If not, then take a moment and close your eyes (go back inside)...help your parts trust that it's safe to let you lead even when the focus is on the outside

Take a few more deep breaths... Begin to become more aware of your outside surroundings... Notice your body in the chair... Move a bit and feel your body, notice the room you are in, come back to this space.

INNER CHILD WORK

The third way to deal with feelings is practicing "Inner Child" work. Most people have heard about the "Inner Child" by now, but who exactly is this so-called Inner Child? Does it truly exist? And why should we care?

As you can imagine, your Inner Child is not a real little baby inside of you. But it is something real- not literally or physically, but figuratively and metaphorically real- and it needs your attention and care. As Stephen Diamond, PhD. (2008), a licensed American clinical and forensic psychologist describes it, "The Inner Child is, like complexes in general, a psychological or phenomenological one. We were all once children, and still have that child dwelling within us. But most adults are quite unaware of this. And this lack of conscious relatedness to our own Inner Child is precisely where so many behavioral, emotional and relationship difficulties stem from." The concept became popular in the writings of Dr. Eric Berne, Dr. Alice Miller, and John Bradshaw in the early 1990's.

Don't get confused or scared; this doesn't mean you suffer from multiple personality disorder (MPD) or Dissociative Identity Disorder (DID). The concept of multiplicity in our minds and inner lives explains this phenomenon. Our psyche is not a unit. It is formed by a series of sub personalities, some of whom we are aware of and some we aren't. The Inner Child is one of them. It is very important to realize that we are not an integrated whole being to ourselves. Our self concept is fractured into a multitude of pieces. In some instances we feel powerful and strong, in others weak and helpless. This is because different parts of us are reacting to different stimuli (different "buttons" are being pushed). The parts of us that feel weak, helpless, needy, etc. are not bad or wrong - what is being felt in those instances is perfect for the reality that was once experienced by the part of our self that is reacting. It was a perfect reaction for *then*, but it does not have the whole perspective with what is happening in the *now*. It is very important to start having compassion for the wounded parts of ourselves. Internal Family Systems Therapy explains this concept at length if you are interested in learning more.

The Inner Child comprises and potentiates our capacity for innocence, wonder, awe, joy, sensitivity and playfulness. But it also holds our accumulated childhood hurts, traumas, fears and angers. As adults we think we have successfully outgrown and left this child (and its emotional baggage) long behind. But this is far from the truth. This is very confusing and hard because people tend to judge themselves for feeling anxious, insecure, afraid, not good enough, lost, small, inferior, and lonely, which are typically feelings of the Inner Child. But if we can recognize this problem for what it is, we can begin dealing with it by choosing to become psychological, not just chronological, adults. How is this accomplished?

First, one becomes conscious of his or her own Inner Child. Remaining unconscious is what empowers the dissociated Inner Child to take possession of the personality at times, to overpower the will of the adult. Next, we learn to take our Inner Child seriously and to consciously communicate with that little girl or boy within, to listen to how he or she feels and what he or she needs from us here and now. The often frustrated primal needs of that perennial Inner Child (for love, acceptance, protection, nurturance, understanding) remain the same today as when we were children. We need to stop trying to make other people fill those needs. Yes, other people can and should help (especially close friends and family and partners) but the main responsibility is on us. It is about collaboration rather than delegation.

Authentic adulthood requires both accepting the painful past and embracing the primary responsibility of taking care of your Inner Child's needs, being a "good enough" parent to him or her, now and in the future. This is why most personal growth work is about re-parenting ourselves. It is ok to be mad, sad, angry and feel all our feelings while going through the stages of grieving our parents' care. Not getting stuck in the grief and doing something different is also key. Now is the time to learn from what you didn't get as a child, what you did get that didn't work for you, and start being your own parent to your Inner Child.

Here is a great exercise from Janae B. Weinhold, PhD. and Barry K. Weinhold, PhD. cited in their book The Flight from Intimacy that will help you identify better the needs of your Inner Child or the developmental stages where he/she is stuck.

EXERCISE: THE SINS OF OMISSION AND COMMISSION

Get a large sheet of paper and divide it into halves, one on the top and the other on the bottom. On the top half, list all the things you wish your parents had said to or done for you that they didn't when you were growing up. (Examples: "I wish they had told me they loved me out loud," "I wish they had given me birthday parties," "I wish they had let me talk on the phone in privacy," "I wish my mom had taught me how to cook.") On the bottom half, list all the things your parents said to you or did to you that you wish they hadn't, things that were in fact hurtful and harmful to you. (Examples: "I wish they hadn't humiliated me when I got pregnant in high school," "I wish they didn't compare me to my sister all the time," "I wish they didn't ground me for participating in extracurricular activities.")

Make your list as long as you like. If you had parent substitutes (such as older siblings, stepparents, or grandparents) as caregivers in your childhood, you may include them, as well as nannies, teachers, scout leaders, coaches or any other significant adults who had a hand in parenting you.

What do these lists mean? The top half, the sins of "omission," identifies the incomplete development forces of your dependent stage. These are the things that leave lifelong patterns of co-dependent behavior. These are the things that the small child in you is still waiting for the perfect parent, the "princess" or the "knight in shining armor" to provide, someone who can read your mind and who knows what you need without you asking. Learning how to complete the incomplete developmental processes represented by the items on this list requires that you take charge of them by finding ways to meet these needs in your life now. The most important skill to learn is to directly ask to get your needs met.

The bottom list, the sins of "commission," identifies the incomplete development processes that helped create your wounds during the process of independence. These wounds can make people flee from intimacy because the small child in you still fears and evades invasive hurtful behaviors from the past. Learning how to complete these processes involves relating unexpressed feelings associated with these early experiences and giving back the things you took that you no longer want or need.

The goal is to relate to the Inner Child exactly as a healthy parent relates to a child, providing discipline, limits, boundaries and structure. These are all (along with support, nurturance, and acceptance) indispensable elements of loving and living with any child, whether metaphorically or actually. By initiating and maintaining an ongoing dialogue between the two, a reconciliation between Inner Child and mature adult can be reached. A new, mutually beneficial, cooperative, symbiotic relationship can be created in which the sometimes conflicting needs of both the adult self and the Inner Child can be creatively satisfied. (Diamond, 2008)

Your Inner Child is an infallible communication center. It lets you know through your feelings what is good or bad for you, when something is right or wrong for you. The point is to start embracing it. For those of you who don't know how to start relating to your Inner Child, here some specific steps:

Compassionately Dialogue with Your Inner Child

Explore your painful feelings, your fears, your false beliefs and the resulting behaviors, and the memories that may cause your pain. Also explore your gifts and what brings joy to your core Self.

Look at this as an exploration into the layers of yourself. Welcome rather than judge or condemn anything that comes up. When you talk to the wounded parts - your angry, hurt, frightened, anxious, numb, shamed, needy, or depressed parts - you ask them to tell you what they feel, and welcome and embrace those feelings, whatever they are. It helps to imagine these feelings as coming from a hurt child or adolescent, and your job is to welcome him or her into your loving embrace so you can learn what you may be doing that causes these painful feelings. Ask this child questions such as, "What am I telling you or doing that is making you feel anxious (or depressed, angry, shamed, etc.)?" "Are you angry at me?" "Do you feel ignored by me?" "How do you feel when I give you food (or drugs, or alcohol, or spend money, etc) when you are feeling lonely, hurt, bored, anxious, depressed or angry?" "What do you really want from me when you are feeling badly?" (Margaret & Chopich, 1990)

Remember, no feelings are ever wrong or bad. All the feelings you have are for good reasons, and by welcoming them with great compassion, you will be able to discover the information these feelings have for you.

The answers will come from deep within you rather than from your head. When you explore anger, fear, loneliness, sadness, depression and anxiety, you are dialoguing with your wounded Self. When you explore what brings you fulfillment, peace and joy, you are dialoguing with your core Self. (Keep in mind that both the wounded Self and the core Self are aspects of your Inner Child.)

A technique I have found very valuable in this healing process is to relate to the different wounded parts of our self as different ages of the Inner Child. These different ages of the child may be literally tied to an event that happened at that age. The age of the child might be a symbolic designator for a pattern of abuse or deprivation that occurred throughout childhood. Some examples are: when I was 7 I remember feeling ridiculed because I couldn't read in front of my class. Or, the 9 year old within me feels completely emotionally isolated and desperately needy and lonely.

The integration process involves consciously cultivating a healthy, loving relationship with your Inner Child and all his stages so that you can love them, validate their feelings, and assure them that everything is different now and everything is going to be all right. As you become aware of the feelings from the child, it might seem like they take over your whole being, like what they say it is the absolute reality. But it isn't- it is just a small part of you reacting out of the wounds from the past. By getting to know, owning and honoring all of the parts of you, you can have a chance to have some balance and union within.

Discover What New, Loving Action You Need to Take on Your Own Behalf

At the end of the day, what we all want is love and acceptance. Check in on what you might be sacrificing your Inner Child for in your attempt to be loved. Identifying what you are willing to trade or lose in order to recover your Inner Child is a huge step.

For example, if you feel somebody isn't being fair to you, your Inner Child might show it to you by feeling angry and sad. However, you might be used to not saying or doing anything for fear of being criticized or not liked. By giving your Inner Child what she needs and letting your inner adult take care of it, you would choose to speak up in an assertive and respectful way so that you can ask for what you need, even if you can't change the outcome. Your Inner Child would feel heard and respected by you independent of what happens in the outside world. You might need to give up the need to "be nice" or "liked" in this situation, but your Inner Child and your overall wellness are worth this sacrifice. In the beginning it is scary and difficult, but once you start experiencing the new reality it becomes a worthy action.

After all, inner bonding is the process of connecting our adult thoughts with our instinctual, gut feelings - the feelings of the "Inner Child" - so that we can minimize painful conflict within ourselves. Free of inner conflict, we feel peaceful, open to joy, and open to giving and receiving love. (Margaret & Chopich, 1990) Another word that describes inner bonding in the psychology literature is called integration. By cultivating the relationship between our adult and Inner Child, we are integrating both sides of our brain (limbic and neurocortex) promoting a more balanced and healthy way of being. By staying with the emotions that come up from the limbic brain, we can calm them and can then access the neurocortex to look for more rational and logical decisions to make.

Establish a Daily Contact/Dialogue

The best way to practice both of these approaches is to try to set a time or times during the day when you can touch base with your Inner Child. With time, it will become a habit and you will no longer need to schedule it. But to start it works best if you establish some regularity. One idea is to set up a reminder on your phone, work computer or next to your bed with the following statement: "Has your adult self spent time with your Inner Child today?"

Since the deepest and most painful feelings usually come from childhood, embracing your Inner Child tends to be very helpful. Here are four specific ways which can help you nurture a connection with your inner life and your Inner Child.

Getting in Touch With Your Inner Child

When people use the common saying of "you have to love yourself before anybody else can love you," they are referring to a process defined by psychologists: earn a secure attachment or an intrapsychic balance (within the individual person) so you can have a healthy relationship with someone else or "relational balance" (interpersonal realm).

When you hear the concept of loving yourself, you can now think of the process of loving your Inner Child (also called parts of you with childlike traits, feelings, and needs). It is especially important to actively do this if you feel unloved, if your Inner Child feels unloved or if you have a profound feeling about your family abandoning, rejecting or neglecting you.

Even though you are ok for the most part, there is a part of your adult self that feels this hurt and pain very acutely sometimes. This pain may flare up quickly in unpredictable ways that are hard for you to control. This part of you is commonly called "the Inner Child" and it may want your attention when you feel down, over-tired or triggered by specific circumstances. The Inner Child will display a lot of childlike emotional behavior such as tantrums, rage, excessive shyness, fear, and strong feelings of not being able to cope. In short, your Inner

Child may react to situations that your adult mind knows are not life or death situations, but your Inner Child views as such.

Your Inner Child often needs a lot of security, nurturing and loving kindness and can act up in times of change and upheaval. Listening to your own needs can be a meditation in itself and if you are upset it is often useful to ask, "What do I need right now?" The answer may be to give yourself something good, such as "I need a cuddle." The answer could also be "I need my family to love me, to listen to me, to see me, to accept me."

Disclaimer: if you suffered significant abuse and/or neglect and the intensity of the feelings is too much, stop this meditation right now. In this situation it is advisable to take this issue to your therapist to work through in depth. You will need expert support.

The answer to "what do I need right now?" could also be something that is not so good for you, such as alcohol, cigarettes, or drugs. As these are things not usually craved by young children, I invite you to dig beyond your inner teenager to a younger you!

Often what the Inner Child craves are basic needs. These are things such as comfort, security, love, affection, warmth, and understanding, especially if these qualities were not abundant in your childhood. Think through how you can give this to yourself. Ask yourself what you found comfort in as a child and what you can find comfort in now. Did you lose yourself in an adventure story, or watching a film? Did you go and play with your friends? If so, what did you do? Did you find comfort outside or inside? In your room or on the street? Where did you find your flow as a child? Was it in writing stories or making gifts for people? Playing sports or cooking? Think about what makes you happy and write it down in your journal. Plan how you can incorporate more of these things into your life. It may mean joining a cookery class or sports club. Perhaps you would like to meet some new people who share similar interests or can give you loving companionship.

Gifts for Your Inner Child

Once in touch with your Inner Child, you may find yourself wanting to give your child the things she wanted but didn't get. This could be anything, like emotional needs such as respect, kindness, love, or a best friend. If your space or independence weren't respected much as a child, you might now need specific physical things such as a safe environment, a room of your own where you can lock the door, a toy you have chosen that no one can take away from you. If you were neglected as a child, perhaps your child needs your full attention, or to have your current needs more fully acknowledged. Perhaps she needs healthier nutrition or a kinder more respectful relationship with her own body.

What were your childhood dreams that were never realized? Maybe you wanted to learn something. Or travel to distant lands. As an adult you are in more of a position to make your childhood dreams come true. Think how satisfied your Inner Child would be if you could do that for yourself.

If you can't give your Inner Child her childhood dream straightaway then you could give a symbol of that gift. For example, if as a child you always wanted to go to Italy, give yourself a flavor of that, such as:

- Make Italian food
- Get a map or a travel book of Italy
- Save up for a trip by putting your money in a Mediterranean style pottery vase
- Plant some basil or marjoram in your garden
- Learn to speak Italian

Inner Child and Nurturing

Awareness of the needs of your inner-child is invaluable. However, part of you may deny your needs because they were denied to a younger you by a dysfunctional upbringing. Sometimes you may display child like behavior and not know why. You may feel extremely upset over a trifle and wonder later why you overreacted. Perhaps your Inner Child craves sugar or affection. Perhaps you crave sex as a way of getting attention, as it was one of the ways you were noticed as a young adult. You could become very angry or crave drugs as a way to numb (deny) what your Inner Child is feeling or as a way to obliterate your strong, painful feelings. Signs that your Inner Child is present might be:

- Feeling extreme childlike emotion like throwing a tantrum
- Feeling abandoned and unable to cope alone
- Not knowing how you feel, as there are too many emotions to concentrate on

- Speaking in absolute terms ("always," "never," "this always happens to me")
- Feeling absolute fear when there is no immediate threat; your fear has been triggered by a TV show or an insensitive comment by someone you love
- Having other strong feelings or extreme negative thoughts about yourself that seemingly came from nowhere (perhaps sparked by a careless remark from a lover or being touched unexpectedly)

If you didn't get your needs met sufficiently when you were very young, your Inner Child may not be able to articulate her feelings in any coherent way. But you may experience strong feelings that you cannot pin-point and have been there as long as you can remember. It may take a lot of practice and awareness to appease your Inner Child. S/he may feel very ignored, hurt, sad angry and frustrated. However s/he feels it is important that you take time to listen to him/her and take his/her feelings into consideration. That is what this practice is all about. LISTEN.

What to Do When Your Inner Child is Acting Up

Find a quite place to relax and tune into yourself. Now try to visualize or get a sense of the place in your own body where your strongest feelings are. Close your eyes and focus on that place inside yourself. Visualize that place inside yourself and take time to notice the color, shape, or texture of your feelings. Then, with loving kindness, endeavor to change these elements to something calmer and more soothing. Ask your Inner Child what she needs and then tell your Inner Child what she needs to hear. This maybe any or all of the following:

- You are safe and loved
- Nothing can harm you now
- It is OK to relax
- I will never leave you
- You are beautiful the way you are
- I will listen to all your feelings, they are ok and they make sense to me
- You have choices now
- You have power now
- You are ok even when other people don't approve your feelings or choices or needs

Visualize where your feelings are in your body again and see if the color or textures have changed. Allow all feelings to come up and be expressed without judgment. Let yourself know that expressing feelings is part of letting go. The overall aim of letting go of feelings is to be free of them so they no longer have such a strong impact on your thoughts and behavior. Do what works for you. However, if your Inner Child is really scared, you need to honor his/her feelings and do more inner work. S/he may be trying to warn you away from self-destructive behavior. Some examples of this would be: being upset after a meaningless sexual encounter, or feeling angry because you didn't say no to your family when s/he wanted you to. Your inner-child can act as a guide to help you change your behavior.

Again, if the feelings are too intense, having the emotional support and presence of a therapist might be the best and more recommendable way to start.

The meditation comes from the 'Nourishment for Difficult Times' website for women survivors of gender based violence: www.healingmeditations.co.uk by Jennifer Weston

STEP TWO: CONNECTING WITH MY COGNITIVE THINKING PATTERNS

IDENTIFYING MY BELIEFS

We are always thinking. What we think isn't always positive. In fact, in his book "The Happiness Trap" author Russ Harris (2008) says that 80 percent of everyone's thoughts contain some sort of negative content. So it's normal to have negative thoughts. It's part of our evolutionary heritage. We're constantly scanning our environment, generating negative thoughts all the while, looking for problems to fix.

Thinking in and of itself isn't the problem. Even a certain amount of negative thinking is necessary. The problem is that when negative thinking is the norm, we don't realize it, and even worse, we believe it. This is when it becomes unhealthy. Lisa Firestone, PhD. (2010) from the Glendone Association & PsyAlive and author of "Conquering Your Inner Voice" calls this phenomenon the "critical inner voice." She refers to the "voices" as a well-integrated pattern of destructive thoughts towards ourselves and others that is at the root of much of our maladaptive behavior. The critical inner voice affects every aspect of our lives, our self-esteem and confidence, and most importantly, our personal and intimate relationships.

This is what happens to people with insecure attachment styles. By default, they tend to generate more negative thoughts according to their style (I will offer more about each style in the next section). We all go about our day to day lives without realizing that there are certain beliefs that play out in the way we interact with ourselves and others. The goal in the following two exercises is to identify some of the basic subconscious beliefs and self-talk that plays out in your head to see if it is helping you to be in a healthy relationship or not. In approaching this area, the key is to develop an inquisitive attitude towards these beliefs- they took years to develop and they seem to us to be absolute truths... but are they really?

EXERCISE #1

Here are some questions to think about that will help you explore some of your basic beliefs:

- What do you typically think about yourself when in a relationship? Do you consider yourself good enough, lovable and loving, deserving, and equal? If you feel you are unequal to your partner, how?

- What do you think about your partner in the relationship? Do you consider s/he is equal or better than you, or not? In what aspects or areas do you feel this way? How and should s/he be different? How does that affect your self-esteem or vision of the

other person?
- What do you think about relationships in general? Are they good or bad? Are they necessary for your existence or not really necessary? Could they be more of a problem?
- What model of relationships were you exposed to during your upbringing?
- What would your mother/father say about your relationship with your partner?
- How would you respond to your mother/father about what they said?
- How do their opinions affect your expectations about yourself, your partner and the concept of relationships?

Thoughts (positive or negative)	Current	New Target (new healthier version if possible)
Thoughts about yourself		
Thoughts about your partner		
Thoughts about the relationship (s)		

As you reflect on these concepts, you may not be able to put what you think into words very easily as these tend to be big underlying concrete concepts (mental constructs) about yourself and the world. So here are some examples of typical negative self-talk and beliefs (Firestone, 2013):

"No one will ever love you. S/he will never care about you. You'll just wind up alone."

"You are just fine on your own. You can take care of yourself. You don't need anyone else. Don't trust him/her."

"I can't get close to you because you will smother me and complicate my life."

"You don't love me unless you validate and meet all my needs."

"I am afraid to depend on you and afraid to want to."

"I can't depend on you."

"People that depend on relationships are weak."

Here is another compilation of typical thoughts most people come up with about themselves: "Nobody listens to me," "I am not important," "I am not worthy enough," "I will lose my freedom," "If I do as others want me to, I will lose myself," "I am not smart," "I can't trust anybody," "I am not lovable," "Nobody will ever want/love me,"

"I am not in control," "It is not ok to feel or show my emotions," "I am a disappointment," "I am not good enough."

I find it helpful here to review the list of typical thought patterns according to your attachment style and complete it if needed:

Anxious Typical Thoughts	**Avoidant Typical Thoughts**	**Other Personal Thoughts You Identify**
Cathastrophizing: This is it. This will never get better. S/he's leaving me.		
	Generalizing: Oh now s/he is going to be telling me what to do all the time, I am never going to see my friends or do my thing again.	
All or nothing thinking: S/he will never call me again. See, s/he doesn't really care.		
	Labeling: S/he is too needy, what is wrong with him/her.	
Generalizing: I will always be alone, nobody takes me seriously.	Dismissive: When did that happen? Did I promise that? Oh it's not that bad…I was just busy.	
Labeling: S/he is so selfish. All s/he		

thinks is about her/himself.

Fortune telling: I knew this was going to happen.

Track keeping: This is the third time s/he does/doesn't do this. It's gotta stop!

Taking it personally: It is because I said or did that. I totally ruined it.

Inferiority complex: It is me again, there is something really wrong with me. I am way too needy and crazy. | Taking it personally: I can't ever do anything right. No matter how much I try, s/he can never be happy.

Inferiority complex: I have to be my best at work, sports, and be in shape so I don't have time for relationships.

Superiority complex: S/he has too many issues for me. I deserve and can get better.

Self focused: If s/he can't accommodate/understand my needs I'd rather be on my own.

Minimizing tendencies: It is not so bad. I don't | |

Superiority complex: What is wrong with him/her. Look at me. Why wouldn't s/he die to be with me?	know why s/he is always so dramatic.
	Forgetful tendencies: I truly don't remember this being so important or you telling me.
Revengeful: Oh you hurt me, fine! So now you are going to see/pay for it.	
	Blame: If you weren't nagging me all the time, things would be ok.
Immediacy: I have to talk/to see him/her right now otherwise I can't be ok.	Fantasize: If s/he was "the right one for me" we wouldn't fight so much. Relationships shouldn't be this hard, so we aren't meant to be. Also fantasize about having sex with other people.
Rumination tendencies: Can't stop thinking about it/s/he. Can't sleep or go back to work until things get resolved.	
	Typical Love knot: "If S/he was "the one," s/he...."
Controlling: Maybe if I look really good	

next time we get back together…If I tell him/her what he/she wants to hear… If I make his/her favorite dinner… Fantasize: Remembering all the good things your partner ever did and said, focusing on all the good traits s/he has. Love knot: "If S/he loved me, s/he would…"		

EXERCISE #2

I like this next exercise because it explicitly articulates the underlying thoughts that some people have but are not in touch with or are too ashamed to verbalize. As you read some of the following examples, try to identify some negative thinking patterns that might be going on when relating them to more specific moments. The following chart is taken from the book "Love Knots: How to Untangle Those Everyday Fights" by Lori Heyman Gordon (1990). It reflects some of the most common examples of thoughts and expectations which create trouble in relationships. With good reason they are called "love mistaken beliefs" or Love Knots. Identify the ones that resonate with you and try to rewrite them into more positive, current, and realistic ones. If you have difficulty accepting the healthier version, coming up with your own, or letting go of the current one, you may benefit from working with a therapist. It might mean that you have deeper wounds to take care of. I have included some blank spaces for you to fill in with your own love knots that come up when being in a relationship. You can also draw from the exercise you just completed above; you may find that there is a love knot linked to some or all of them.

Love Knot	**Healthier Option**	**Your Own Version**
If you loved me, you would know what I feel, think and would want and would give it to me. Since you	I cannot assume that you know. I will ask for what I want and not expect you to know or give me everything.	

don't, you obviously don't care.		
If you loved me you would agree with me, you would want what I want and like what I want. Since you don't, you don't love me. If you loved me, you wouldn't try to change me. You don't love me for what I am.	We are all unique and different. Agreement or disagreement doesn't necessarily indicate love or the lack of it. Differences can be discussed, understood, changed, or accepted.	
If you love me you would bring excitement and new experiences into my life. You would plan and make them happen. Since you don't you must not feel I am worthy doing that for. You must not love me.	Part of our uniqueness is that we are drawn to different things. I must take responsibility from bringing things that I want up or make them happen and not use your initiative as a test of my worth or your love for me.	

If you loved me you would find me attractive and you would tell me so and want to be close to me. If you don't you don't love me.	When you don't find me attractive I cannot assume I know why. I will ask for the information I need, check out my perceptions and not assume.	
If I were important to you, you would remember what I tell you. You don't think what I have to say is important; you don't think I am important, you don't love me.	I will keep in mind that even when you listen you might be distracted, preoccupied or forget. I will try to get your full attention and remind you if needed a decent amount of times decided by both of us. Your ability to remember isn't necessarily a reflection of your feelings for me. When in doubt, I will ask and not assume.	
Your Own Love Knots		

CONNECTING MY BELIEFS WITH MY FEELINGS

All of the beliefs and thoughts you uncovered in the previous section may be generated internally or by an external event happening. In reality, it doesn't matter since in the end, any thought or belief is usually connected to a feeling (or vice versa) in a process that happens in a thousandth of a second, which is the basic premise of well-known Cognitive Behavioral Therapy (CBT) modality. So try filling out this chart adjusted from CBT to become more aware of the connection between your thoughts and feelings.

THOUGHTS & FEELINGS DAILY LOG

Emotion/Feeling	Level 0-10	Describe the event internal or external that trigger the emotion (if not identifiable, leave blank)	What are you thinking the moment you are feeling the emotion(s)?	Distortions of Thoughts (not 100% real)	Positive Thoughts: Substitute new thoughts that are positive, real, valid.	Level 0-10
Sadness or depression	10	Boyfriend didn't call, break up; your wife criticized you; date didn't follow through; partner forgot your request…	You may tell yourself: I will never be happy without ___. You will **always** be alone. Nobody will ever listen to you.			5
Guilt or shame						
Frustration						
Anger						
Anxiety or worry						
Fear or panic						
Loneliness or abandonment						
Hopelessness, discouragement						
Other						

*It could be the events, feelings, or thoughts that initiate the cycle. Do not let the format to confuse you. If in your case the thought or event happened first, start filling out the columns in that order. That is not important. What matter is that you fill out each one of them at then end.

Adjusted from Cognitive Behavioral Therapy

Once you identified your main feelings (typically one or two per situation) try to find out if there is a subconscious automatic thought that tends to come up with that feeling. Remember that these thoughts tend to belong to three main general categories: yourself, your partner or the world (pull from exercise above). At times, it can also be a thought that triggers the feelings, so the order doesn't matter, but try to identify the main connections that come up for you. We all tend to have a few that are our main themes and triggers, and different situations just revolve around them.

Now, try to do a reality check and see if in the current situation those thoughts are accurate. Check for words with an absolute connotation such as "always," "never," "nobody," and "should." Also check for labeling (stupid, loser, the best, only...), generalizing, taking the negative out of proportion, and all-or-nothing thinking. Most of the time, there can be some truth in your negative thoughts, but in general they are not as extreme or dangerous as the original statements reflect. Now see if you can lower the intensity of your feelings based on your new and hopefully more objective view of the situation. Also check for situations where your feelings might be too low, delayed, or non-existent and see if that is congruent or incongruent with the event (this is mostly applicable for avoidant style).

If you get stuck with intense feelings and negative thoughts and you can't seem to be able to decrease their intensity or change them by following these steps, you might benefit from individual therapy. Also, if you aren't clear about what a healthy emotional reaction should be, doing some work with a therapist is also recommended.

All of these discoveries offer a new glimpse into successful relationships, providing the keys to identifying and repairing old wounds that we all have, learning to treat them in a different and healing way in ourselves and in others. Keep in mind that the key is to try to get yourself into the optimal window of emotional arousal and then insert a new and more realistic thought to break the old negative pattern.

STEP THREE: TAKING ACTION TOWARDS CHANGE

And now the most important step: ACTION. If you were able to decrease the intensity of your feelings and do not feel too emotionally detached or shut down (some people describe it as "not feeling anything"), if your negative thoughts aren't your absolute truth and you are open to a new way of being, now is the best opportunity to change your spontaneous reactions. Now is your opportunity to create new behavioral options that can get you what you want, taking into consideration your new view, your feelings, situation and needs as well as your partner's or other people involved. Keep in mind that this is never a totally perfect process, which is true of most real life situations. Try to do the opposite of what you are used to doing. For example, if you usually sacrifice your needs and please others, try to be true to your needs. By default, if you in general put yourself first, try to put others' needs first in certain scenarios. By pairing a new behavior/reaction with the appropriate range of emotion and a new version of the thought, you are creating a new pathway in your brain. With new and different reactions to old feelings and thoughts you can create new healing possibilities for yourself and for others. You will see some examples of healthy reactions to common insecure patterns further down in this chapter.

Now is the time to relate all that you have learned so far with your *attachment style*! All of us have common reactions when in relationships. Most of your common feelings, thoughts and actions will be typical of your attachment style. The purpose now is to find out which ones specifically fall within the realm of an insecure style as they are probably hindering you from having healthy fulfilling relationships the most. Remember that since most people don't fit exclusively within one quadrant, they may present secure reactions at times. However, if your test results showed an insecure attachment style, focus on which ones are frequently present, as well as how often. Obviously the more frequent, the stronger the style.

We have already covered the thoughts and emotions categories in the sections above. So here is a third category of reactions which illustrate the most common ways each type of insecure style manifests itself. Mark the ones you identify with the most:

Common Anxious Reactions

- Pursues
- Protest behavior
- Initiates communication most of the time
- Initiates fights or conflict
- Wants to talk about emotions, sometimes in an excessive way
- Shows affection, caring behaviors, and physical touch most of the time
- Wants things done in a certain way
- Shows and provokes jealousy
- Tends to be open, generous and giving, sometimes too much
- Tends to alternate between aggressiveness and passivity

- Reacts quickly; sometimes acts impulsively
- Can be paralyzed and need a lot of external direction/ validation
- Withdraws love when feeling hurt
- Keeps in mind/includes partner in personal life/activities, sometimes in an excessive way
- Typical love knot: "If s/he loved me, s/he ..."

Common Avoidant Reactions

- Runs away
- Disconnect/deactivate behavior
- Avoids or doesn't initiate communication most of the time
- Stays away from fights or conflict in general
- Criticizes other's feelings or actions
- Denies and looks down on vulnerable feelings (insecurity, jealousy, fear, loneliness...)
- Tends to be self centered, withholding affection; doesn't initiate physical closeness
- Tends to alternate between passive-aggressive and dominant/controlling behavior
- Tends to take defensive position
- Keeps information and emotional sharing to a minimum
- Doesn't share feelings or emotions; sticks to the facts
- Tends to freeze and rejects external direction
- Withdraws loves when hurt
- Typical love knot: "If s/he was 'the one,' s/he...."

(Adapted from Attached, 2010)

Look back at your Attachment Style answers from the questionnaire on page 22 and the sheets from Exercises 1 and 2 from Part One of Chapter Three on pages 36 and 38. It is time to compare and/or add any statements to the following list that you consider appropriate to create your personal work list.

Here is an example of a personal work sheet:

Common thoughts	Common emotions	Common behaviors	Attachment style (if you can identify it or them)

To deepen your awareness and go a step further, you can also identify particular common situations that tend to stress your particular attachment style and think of ways to take care of yourself in those moments. Ask your partner for help to do, not do, say or not say what you know will help decrease the stress. For example, a typical situation may arise between a person with anxious style and a person with avoidant style where they need to talk over a problem and resolve a conflict. If the person with avoidant style doesn't want to engage or needs some space, the person with anxious style could ask for a specific time to resume the conversation. Asking for a particular time to reunite will help calm down feelings of abandonment or invalidation. The same principle applies for the person with avoidant style. If their partner's need to talk suffocates him, owning it, naming it and asking for some specific space can take care of that. Keep in mind that asking for some time is different that closing down and not wanting to talk at all. So this is a classic example of changing behavior. Person A didn't persist in

> "Perhaps the single greatest advance in psychological and social theory in the last 50 years has been the emergence of family systems- thinking. In intimate systems, such as family, all parties play dovetailed roles. The bumps on her head fit the holes in his hand. An alcoholic wife requires an enabling husband, a rebellious teenager requires a family that avoids its problems by designating him the patient, the women 'who loves too much' requires a 'dance-away lover'."
>
> Sam Keen
>
> *Fire in the Belly*

talking right now about everything and person B didn't run away and not talk at all. The resolution is a balanced middle ground that resembles the behavior of people with secure attachment style. This case is typical as it is common for one partner to not want to talk over things immediately and the other to want to solve it all right there and then. Remember that the lifelong goal is not to judge, and to accept with compassion you and your partner's process (thoughts and feelings from your old brain) while continuing to embrace the idea that you both have a journey that feeds from each other.

At this stage, new situations may have come to your mind after completing the work in this section. If you feel like it, you can go back to the list of frustrations in Chapter Three on page 42 and add to it. This would also be a good time to complete the fourth column of the PAIRS exercise on page 44. Again, if you have some trouble coming up with healthy enough suggestions, you might benefit from some therapy to help you get through certain blocks. Struggling with this is normal so don't worry too much if that is your case.

Here are some examples of scenarios from common situations and how you can make improvements towards a healthy way to respond together:

1. It is a common work week. Both partners are busy and tired with work and daily chores. The person with anxious attachment starts to feel down or angry. Her common reactions would be to start asking for reassurance in an indirect way ("Do you love me?" "Do you find that woman attractive?" "What is

so interesting in your computer?") or criticizing her partner ("You are so self centered"... "Fine, we always do what you want to do anyway"... "Another trip with your friends; I thought we didn't have enough money?") The person with avoidant style won't see anything wrong and may start explaining how busy things are and start criticizing the feelings of the other person ("You are so dramatic"... " I am tired of your drama"... "Enough of it, I don't want to talk about it again and again").

A new version would involve the same feelings but with a different approach:

The person with anxious style communicates to her partner that she started to feel disconnected and would like to either spend some time together or needs some words of affirmation or...Then person with avoidant style would validate her feelings, saying something like "Thank you for pointing it out. You are right, we have not been able to spend much time together but I still have to finish this project. How about I take a break so we can do something together now, and then let's plan something else for Friday night when I will be done? I do love you and I know it is important for us to spend quality time together as well."

2. Two partners are attending a social event. The person with anxious style might start feeling insecure or lonely while the person with avoidant style socializes with friends and other

people. After all, that is why they are attending the event! Common reactions would be for the anxious partner to start analyzing every single one of their partner's behaviors, trying to find faults or reasons to blame her, maybe calling her over for a talk or even needing to leave the party. The person with avoidant style would start defending and explaining that they are there to socialize and that he should do the same and leave her alone, after emphasizing that he shouldn't start with his "dramas."

The new version would be: "Hey honey, are you having a good time? I am also enjoying chatting with friends but would also like to spend some time with you. Would you like to join me for a drink or dance a couple of songs together?" The person with avoidant style would say "Sure, let me finish with Mike and I will meet you at the bar in five minutes!" Most importantly, they would follow through and meet their partner with enthusiasm. The person with anxious style might then say thank you and go on and find another friend to socialize, giving his partner some space, or they may decide to mutually do that together.

3. Two people are dating. A few months into the relationship one person starts feeling that the other isn't paying as much attention to them as in the beginning, that he is too focused on his work, TV, or friends (which by then, might be somewhat true). So a typical anxious person would start making negative

comments about his friends or show or work instead of stating her needs. And with good reason: if she becomes vulnerable and shares that she is probably feeling a little abandoned or not so important, her worst fear might come true. The avoidant partner would judge her feelings and dismiss them as exaggerated, not true and embarrass her for being too needy.

The new healthier version to prevent that cycle would be: the anxious person would articulate what her fears or needs are (such as needing more time together, reassurance, words...) The person with avoidant style, instead of feeling judged or wrong, listens, doesn't judge, stop what he is doing and creates some space to respond to his partner's needs. He would validate her feelings, respond in an empathic way, and then reassume his tasks, work, hobbies or friends.

It is helpful in these situations to try to find a middle ground as there is often truth in both perspectives. If somebody is feeling abandoned, it is partly because of personal stuff but also partly because the other person is too disconnected, which is triggering the abandonment neuropathway. In the same way, if somebody is feeling engulfed, it is partly because of personal stuff but also partly because the other person is insisting or pursuing too much. It takes two to tango, so we cannot say that somebody is being totally needy without another person's response or totally dismissive in a vacuum.

"Perhaps the single greatest advance in psychological and social theory in the last 50 years has been the emergence of family systems-thinking. In intimate systems, such as family, all parties play dovetailed roles. The bumps on her head fit the holes in his hand. An alcoholic wife requires an enabling husband, a rebellious teenager requires a family that avoids its problems by designating him the patient, the women "who loves too much" requires a "dance-away lover."

Fire in the Belly- Sam Keen

Your chart:

Situation	Old thought, emotion, behavior	New thought, emotion, behavior
Boyfriend is out and said he was going to call.	He might be with somebody else. Jealousy. Start calling no stop.	He might be busy, having fun and forgot to call. It doesn't mean he doesn't love/care about me. Somewhat disappointed. Distract yourself and do something else.
Girlfriend asks me to get together when	She is so needy. I don't know if I can take it. Overwhelmed,	She loves me and wants to spend time together,

I am very busy at work.	engulfed. Withdrawn, shut down, don't answer phone.	what is wrong with that? It makes sense. Warmth and happiness. Apologized for not being able to meet and offer other options for spending time together.

It is important to emphasize that there are pros and cons about each attachment style; no style is bad or worse than the other. It is mostly a matter of each person individually tuning down or up their emotional reactions, expanding or reducing themselves, and redirecting the focus of their perspectives (emotions or facts) so they can become more balanced separately and then together. Instead of being a yin and yang by being polarized entities, each person becomes one on their own and then merges with the other.

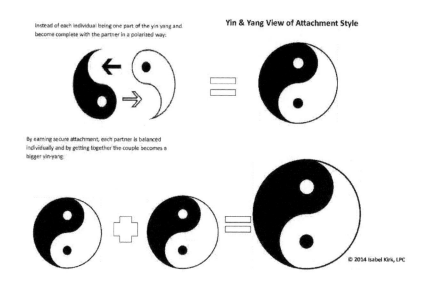

In this way, it is crucial to be aware of what you tend to do or become that blinds you in moments of stress or conflict, and taking advantage of the qualities that you and your partner can bring each into the picture.

When coping with stress, anxious individuals tend to use emotions as their main tool and tend to sustain them or even exaggerate them. The downside of this is that they tend to overemphasize the feeling of *helplessness* and *vulnerability* which usually interferes with their ability to problem-solve and increases the experience of negative emotions about their self and the world. Anxious individuals have a poor ability to suppress separation-related thoughts and become disorganized by the intensity of their ruminating and catastrophic nature. It becomes detrimental to the individual and the relationship.

However, they also tend to be more intuitive and able to detect subtle information. They tend to be more empathic and supportive of their partner's distress.

On the other hand, avoidant individuals in a stressful situation tend to detach and rely on distancing which is also problematic for the individual and the relationship. The person tends to lose a sense of connectedness which helps maintain trust and dependency on others to achieve emotional regulation, and they take longer to regulate themselves. Moreover, avoidant people tend to view negative emotions and expression of weakness or vulnerability as incompatible with their desire for self-reliance. In their effort to maintain a deactivated attachment system, they tend to promote problem solving and disregard emotions. In this way, they refuse to care for and support their distressed partner which usually elicits more anger in the anxious partner. However, they are also able to remain more steady during troubled times and their problem solving is more effective when it is needed.

Anxious people tend to retrieve more painful memories from childhood and overreact to situations that might not be a threat but are perceived in their cognitive structure as such. Avoidant people tend to block painful memories or record fairly shallow ones. They present low levels of self-reported anger while having high levels of physiological arousal and facial expressions.

Here are some additional questions to deepen your awareness about how you react during conflict:

- How do I place my grievances with my partner, or how do I typically pick a fight?
- What is my partner's typical fighting style?
- In what ways do I "fight dirty" with my partner?
- What is my usual psychological state when I pick a fight?
- Do I typically make-up after a fight? How?
- What do I especially like about my fighting style as it now is?
- What aspects of my conflict style do I think get in the way of me having better relationship(s)? Why?
- What would I like to change about my style?

STEP FOUR: CULTIVATING A SECURE ATTACHMENT

"Interdependence is a higher value than independence. Effectiveness requires us to be collaborative, deliberative, cooperative and principled."

Steven Covey, *7 Habits of Highly Effective People*

WHAT SECURE ATTACHMENT LOOKS LIKE

Since our goal is to bring you closer to secure relational attachment, it is time to introduce you to what Secure Attachment looks like. This is the answer to a question millions of people ask: "what do *normal* people do or feel?" Well, we won't get into the discussion about what "normal" and "not normal" is, since normal is more about the amount of people that do something or look a certain way than about the quality of the point in question. Instead, we can take a look at how *healthy* people function, which is what we truly want to achieve.

As Deany Laliotis, LICSW and EMDR Institute Senior Trainer sustained (2014), securely attached individuals have the capacity to feel their internal world while also being able to have interpersonal relationships without sacrifice of self or others. They have the capacity to both feel and deal with life's problems, while being in relationship with others.

Securely attached people tend to promote communication and closeness while still allowing for separation times. Because they are healthily in tune with their own feelings and needs, they can also acknowledge and validate their partner's and are able to compromise changes that benefit the relationship without losing themselves.

A secure attachment style is very important because it significantly determines our ability to build or maintain successful relationships and be healthy, happy and balanced in life. Why? Because attachment is responsible for:

- shaping the success or failure of future intimate relationships
- the ability to maintain emotional balance
- the ability to enjoy being ourselves and to find satisfaction in being with others
- the ability to rebound from disappointment, discouragement, and misfortune

A secure attachment shapes our brain. It makes sense, doesn't it? If people have a healthy brain (with the ability to access both emotions and logic) they are able to be alone and intimate at the same time, maintain an appropriate level of emotional arousal (not too distressed, not too numb) and are able to maintain a positive view of themselves, others and the world even when in adversity.

People wonder how we can be so affected today for something that happened so long ago, or fear that we are just blaming our parents. The short answer is that it is not the parent's fault. It is simply a fact that early relationships affect the way the brain develops, and that is why the effects last for a life time unless intervention takes place.

Scientific study of the brain and the role attachment plays in shaping it has given us a new basis for understanding why vast numbers of people have great difficulty communicating with the most important individuals in their work and love lives. In the past, we could only guess to try and determine why important relationships never evolved, developed chronic problems, or fell apart. Now, thanks to new insights into brain development, we can understand what it takes to help build and nurture productive and meaningful relationships at home and at work.

According to Dianne Poole, PhD (2015), Trauma and Adult Attachment Model expert, there are 8 pillars of secure attachment:

- Basic physical and emotional safety.
- Presence (empathy + attunement): there has to be enough

physical time as well as emotional presence when together.
- Easy flow between connection with others and solitude. In other words, there is a capacity for being interdependent (not over-depending on people, nor over-valuing independency or auto-sufficiency).
- Trust: a basic feeling that people (themselves and others) and the world are good in general. They consider themselves deserving of respect and love.
- Positive holding environment: no chaos or violence, not too much or too little stimulation, and enough responsiveness.
- Capacity to repair after disruption happens (people are capable of giving and receiving apologies, validating feelings, and intending to not repeat hurtful behavior).
- Predictability and consistency: you can relax in the relationship, there is presence of person (parent or partner brings affect regulation) and there is (for the most part) security that the person is there for me.
- Language: Capacity for effective communication (so called assertiveness).

When people grow up or live in an environment with these characteristics, they naturally develop a secure attachment style. For people without that luck, because attachment styles are fluid and can change, a secure attachment can be earned in a healthy relationship with a partner or a therapist.

Characteristics of Securely Attached People (Levine & Heller, 2010):

- Get in touch with what is bothering them
- Have appropriate range of emotion: not too overwhelmed, not shut down
- Communicate their feelings while attending to partners' needs
- Believe they are worthy of love and affection and expect partners to be responsive and caring
- Take other people's needs and preferences into account, even when they oppose their own
- Find it easier to understand partners perspective and maintain focus on the problem

If we could represent graphically the types of attachment it would be as follows:

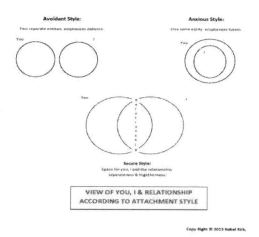

SECURE COMMUNICATION SKILLS

One of the main areas where people manifest their attachment problems is in their communication. Whenever a couple sees me for therapy and I ask about what brings them in, the typical answer is: "We are having some 'communication problems'." They say so because they can't really explain what is going on. They can see the symptom but not the cause, so that is what they think the problem is. The way somebody communicates is influenced by their beliefs, defenses, emotions, needs... in other words, by their attachment style. So when one person's is polarized with the other, you can imagine things don't go very well and "talking over each other" happens. Let's take a look and see how securely attached people go about communicating. When it comes to re-molding our attachment style, the more we practice certain skills the more secure attachment can become second nature. This is what is called in therapy "earned secure attachment."

> *"Loving partners find effective ways of dealing with their differences. They do not view each encounter as a battle to be won or lost."*
> Susan Forward, PhD

Effective communication works on the understanding that we all have very specific needs in relationships, many of which are determined by our attachment style. They aren't good or bad, they simply are what they are. If you are anxious, you have a strong need for closeness and to constantly be reassured that your partner loves you and respects you. If you are avoidant, you need to be able to maintain some distance, either emotional or physical, from your partner and preserve a larger degree of separation.

In order to be happy in relationships, we need to find a way to communicate our attachment needs clearly without resorting to attacks or defensiveness. (Levine & Heller, et al., p. 222) Effective communication is the most powerful tool secure people use in everyday life. The good news is that these skills can be learned.

> People look to close relationships for psychological support, mutual intimacy, and emotional involvement. Communication skills that foster these affective functions are therefore particularly valued in close relationships. (Samter & Burleson, 1990) Burleson and Samter (1990; also see Samter & Burleson, 1990) developed the Commu - nication Functions Questionnaire (CFQ) to describe evaluations of six affective communication skills (comforting, ego-support, expressivity, listening, behavioral regulation, conflict management) and four instrumental skills (conversing, informing, persuading, narrating).
>
> Two affective communication skills that seem to be particularly important in close relationships are comforting and ego support. (Burleson et al, 1996; Burleson & Samter, 1990, 1996) Comforting skills involve the ability to make depressed or sad people feel better, whereas ego-support concerns the ability to make others feel good about themselves. Research on

attachment style differences in social skills suggests that two additional affective skills, expressiveness (the ability to disclose thoughts and feelings) and listening, are crucial in the context of emotional support in close relationships because these skills target the elaboration and processing of emotional experiences. Guerrero, 1996; Guerrero & Jones, 2003 (as cited in Jones, 2005, p. 236)

Given the crucial role that communication plays in attachment and life, I am going to offer some action steps that you can start to practice to help yourself earn a more secure attachment style. But before I do, I want to explain how important it is that certain conditions are in place. Based on my experience, most people with insecure attachment style are afraid of being vulnerable and direct. They aren't in touch with what they feel or need deep down, and mostly resort to what doesn't work. And this makes sense. If they are who they are today, it is because their experiences in past relationships weren't validating enough, they were criticized a lot or felt guilty for having the needs they had. Therefore, they learned unhealthy ways to try and communicate because the main purpose was usually to protect themselves, to not show or feel or need "too much," and to look "ok" or "right." In other words- to survive. When people are in survival mode, they are unable to healthily connect.

Therefore, the most important ingredient to have before attempting to apply the following principles is to make sure the elements for a secure holding environment as described above by Dianne Poole, PhD. on page 98 are there. Otherwise, the exposure will be hurtful and retraumatizing and the person won't want to open up or try ever again. In other words, if someone decides to express their feelings honestly, as secure effective communication will suggest, but the partner or family member listening doesn't understand their part in the equation and what this new style of communication is about, criticism or invalidation will inevitable happen. It is true that we can only control ourselves, but because we are dealing with attachment injuries and trying to heal them, it would be almost impossible to walk away feeling satisfied by only doing your part.

In certain situations you may not think you will see much progress in terms of attachment repair, and walking away is all you can do as a last option. Sometimes it is what it is. By at least learning the principles I am going to share, you will be able to recognize when other people aren't following them, which will explain and validate your feelings and help you to avoid feeling guilty and confused as you did in the past.

In order to create a safe holding environment with your partner, you need to apply the concept of "what can I do for you in order for you to help me." In matters of attachment, we trigger each other's survival mechanisms; by staying aware of what sends a danger signal to your partner's brain, we can do less of that trigger, do something different, or acknowledge it so it loses intensity.

Before we go deeper into secure communication principles, the following lists are things to keep in mind when communicating according to your style:

Anxious Style (pursuer)

- When expressing your feelings, announce in advance if you don't need/ want things to be changed right away, but just need to be listened to.
- When describing negative situations, try to use fewer extreme adjectives.
- If you feel like generalizing or catastrophizing, consider introducing the following sentence: "It might not be the total reality, but to me it feels like..."
- Pick up on the verbal/ non-verbal cues from your partner that trigger you and try to identify what he or she could do differently. For example: "When you use the words 'just...' or 'you are doing a great job' or 'everything will be ok' it makes me feel unheard or that you don't get me, and I start feeling angry."
- By having done the work in previous chapters, you could easily identify what you need and then try to express it in a calm way. For example: "What I need to hear from you is .... or to know that you see how difficult this is, that it is so scary or frustrating or unfair etc."
- Keep the anger and intensity of feelings a little under control- not because the feelings are wrong but so that your partner can stay present and connected.

Avoidant Style (distancer)

- When feeling overwhelmed or shut down by *another* conversation, try to stay positive, open and agree to talk and stay connected.
- When offering your point of view, recognize the negative aspects of the situation before pointing out positive aspects or solutions. Use feelings words.
- Stay with the other person's feelings without judging or trying to make sense of them. Remind yourself that they are just feelings, notice your reaction to them, and embrace them anyway. If they are too much, share your emotional reaction with your partner.
- Pick up on the verbal/ non-verbal cues from your partner that trigger you and try to identify what he or she could do differently. Ex. When you use the word "disaster" or "things will never get better" or "I never do... "It makes me feel scared that we are both going to drown in negativity and not come out or that I can never make you happy.
- Having done the work in previous chapters, you could easily identify what you need and then try to express it in a calm way. For example: "I am beginning to disconnect or shut down from you…" or "I know it has been pretty bad, but can you also try to see that sometimes (like yesterday when I did what you asked) things are ok and that we can find solutions together?" etc
- If you need a break or aren't available in the moment, explain

your feelings (not so much the external situation because it might sounds like an excuse) and announce the reconnection time. For example: "Can we talk after I have a shower, or after dinner, or first thing tomorrow morning?" Try to keep in within 24 hours so your partner can stay within the optimal window of arousal.
- Keep in touch with your own feelings and partner's as much as possible.

After these preparation steps, you will be more ready to apply the following secured attached communication principles.

Principles of Secure Effective Communication

When observing people or couples who are securely attached, there are certain principles or elements that their communication presents. Try to follow them as much as possible until they become second nature for you.

1. Reflection

    Before talking, think about the issue instead of addressing it reactively or defensively in the moment.

2. Active Listening:

    - Face the speaker and maintain eye contact to show attentiveness.
    - Wait until the speaker is done before disagreeing, defending, assuming you know what he or she is going to

say.

- Let go of details or specific words and continue to try to get the main message.
- Try to not be thinking about what you are going to say next.
- Keep an open mind and continue to be engaged by asking questions and seeking clarification.
- Try to avoid *why* questions. You are simply requesting a fuller description of the feelings.
- Avoid the tendency to "fix" or have your partner "explain" his or her feelings. Your goal is to understand the phenomenon of your partner's feelings with true empathy, to walk for a moment in your partner's shoes. When you feel that you have understood your partner's feelings, let them know: "I think I understand how you feel."

3. "I" Statements

Begin sentences with mostly "I" and use feelings words.

4. Objectivity

Focus on objective information when relating stories about your partner or describing their behavior. Avoid all or nothing words such as "always", "never" or qualifying adjectives towards the other person such as "selfish" "dramatic" "lazy" etc.

5. No Mind Reading

Avoid mind-reading statements such as "you don't care" or "you didn't like it" and use more open ended questions such as "I had the impression you didn't like ... is that the case? Tell me more."

6. Be Present

   Focus on the now and on the present situation. Avoid generalizing the conflict.

7. Clarity

   Be direct, clear and specific about your needs, wants or requests for change.

8. Internal Validation

   Secure individuals know their requests are valid because they need them and don't have to be justified according to what is "right," what "most people do," or how it "should be" etc.

9. Empathy

   Feel and show concern for the other person's well-being; try to give the person what they are looking for: validation, listening, brainstorming, possible solutions, comfort...

10. Win-Win

    Look for win-win resolutions and check for feelings and reconnection at the end. Keep in mind that in reality, not every situation presents a 50-50% resolution, but more like 60-40%. Try to look at the big picture and see if you and your partner tend to alternate the 60-40% so you both feel you win in the end.

You may be feeling overwhelmed and ask: how can some people do all of this? In the beginning, this will be a lot to focus on! Preparing a Dialogue Script for your message is recommended so you can incorporate these elements at a manageable pace.

Steps for Writing a Script Message (10 minutes)

1. Time the writing. Try to do it after you get some distance from the situation and your feelings are within the optimal zone arousal (not too charged, not too numb).

2. Begin by asking yourself "How do I feel about…?" or "How do I feel when…?" and write it at the top of your page (for a reference you can go back and check list of your relationships frustrations).

3. In the body of the message, address the question, focus on feelings and describe your feelings fully ("I feel like…"). There are no right or wrong answers.

4. Try to find out the physical sensations in your body, the inner dialogue or story you might be making, or the memory or past experience. Use this form for the first several weeks to help structure your response.

5. Get in touch with what you need and try to be as specific as possible in terms of time, place, how and frequency. If possible

try to present options so if something doesn't work right away or your partner can't accommodate /respond to your first request, there are other possibilities for your needs to be met.

6. When ready, ask your partner or other person for a dialogue.

7. Announce your intentions about it and ask for active listening skills (look at secure attachment style principles of communication). If needed go over them together before the conversation as a gentle reminder.

8. As the initiator, seek to stay with description vs. explanations (do not apologize for having the feeling, justify the feeling, try to figure out why you have the feeling etc). When you feel that your partner has understood your feelings let him or her know that ("You seem to understand my feelings").

9. If resolution isn't achieved, or the best way to proceed isn't agreed upon, try to relax and let the conversation be for now. It is important to give some time to the other person to resolve his/her own feelings about the exchange and process information. You might reunite later if he/she needs to share his/her reactions and/or look for other possible solutions.

10. Thank your partner/other person and then try to occupy yourself and your mind in something else. Otherwise, it won't be productive.

Over time and with practice, your responses will happen more automatically. Remember also that the foundation work of the previous chapters has begun the healing journey of re-shaping your attachment style. Without the continued healing of this foundational work, your attempts at changing your communication only may fail. You will only end up feeling more frustrated and guilty for not being able to follow through. You may have experienced this with other books in the past. People have told me: "It is not that I don't know *what* to do, I just can't apply it in the moment!"

My encouragement to you is to do the work of the previous sections and start to practice new communication skills at the same time. You don't have to wait until you have a perfectly secure attachment before you act differently. You will need to practice to get it. I even recommend preparing yourself privately before communicating so you can get a hold of your difficulties and more consciously apply the skills mentioned above. It will also be too difficult in the beginning to apply all of this in the middle of a huge conflict, so start practicing with less intense issues when your brain is more integrated (more capable of being in touch with you and your partner's emotions and needs, while remembering logical information and being able to problem solve).

Over time, you will start to see these characteristics of secure attachment growing in yourself and will be able to do all of this as second nature:

1. Be able to feel emotion and be logical at the same time

2. Be able to keep in mind both you and your partner's needs

3. Be confident about your needs and feelings as much as you are open and not critical of others

4. Be willing and open to consider other points of views and ways

5. Be able to deal with adversity while continuing to be engaged and problem solve

Now, if communication turns into conflict (which is inevitable and part of life), there are certain downfalls each attachment style tends to default to. I will describe them here so you can be aware of what may be happening when you experience these behaviors.

Typical reactions from Avoidant Style

- Brushes off
- Makes other person feel needy, inadequate, foolish
- Responds to the other person only factually and doesn't take emotions into consideration
- Cannot get in touch with what is really bothering them

The best way to counteract these behaviors is to realize when you are ready to withdraw. Mention it and do or ask for what you need to in order to remain engaged with yourself or your partner. It is ok still to take some time alone. Try to decrease or do fewer things that activate disengagement. Announce a specific time to reconnect (if in a relationship) and try to keep it within twenty-four hours.

Typical reactions from Anxious Style

- Flooded with emotions
- Black and white thinking
- Protest behavior
- Wants to solve it all

The best way to counteract these behaviors is to realize when you are turning to protest behavior. Mention it and do or ask for what you need in order to maintain control with yourself or partner. Remember the techniques and examples suggested in the communication preparation steps above for each style, and ask your partner to slow down so that you can get some validation of your feelings and/or physical regulation if appropriate (hug, hold hands, eye gaze…)

In all of this, remember that your relationship needs are valid. Period. Most people wonder if they are too much, if they are being over reactive and are afraid of being vulnerable. The truth is that statistics show that around 50% of the population is going through some or many of these areas of growth. If you can own them, accept them, and learn to love yourself and your partner wherever you find yourselves, you can work things out for the better. If you are defensive, trying to present yourself with no flaws, feeling offended and wanting to hide when somebody notices or mentions these things, you may get stuck and continue to fail in your relationships. Also, if you continue to think your partner is the only one with issues and you refuse to look at yourself and your role in the relationship, you may continue to fail in your relationships also. When people point certain things out, ask them to be gentle and treat you with compassion while helping you to heal those wounds. You can compassionately offer to help them heal theirs as well; you can both help each other. It may seem easier said than done (I know!) but you can do it!

Throughout life, both men and women need someone who is available (will be there) and responsive (when I need you). This is the bottom line of relationship security in attachment. (Johnson, 2010).

So let's take a look at how your understanding of secure attachment is going so far. Look over the following scenarios and see if you agree with the style answers or if you are surprised by them:

Boyfriend calls and announces that he will be coming home late. Midnight happens and he is not home yet.

Reactions:
- Girlfriend watches TV and doesn't even notice/ remember that it is late and boyfriend hasn't showed up nor has called. (Avoidant style)
- Girlfriend notices time, that it is late and that boyfriend hasn't called or arrived. Wonders what is going on but thinks he should call or be home soon or will explain later what happened and goes to bed. (Secure style)
- Girlfriend is checking the clock and door and starts wondering what is wrong with him. She tries to watch TV or go to bed but can't because now her mind is racing and thinking something bad happened or boyfriend is cheating on her. (Anxious style)

Which one did you think was ok and which one are you more similar to?

Another fun way to continue to exercise your brain towards a secure attachment (whether you are in a relationship or not) is to think of possible scenarios like the one above or look at real situations around you and imagine how you would feel, think and react. Look around and start seeing with the new attachment lens how people in movies, friends, family members or characters in books relate to each other. Then see how close or far it is from what secure attachment looks like. Of course, try to imitate the ones that look more like the secure ones.

FINAL SUGGESTIONS AND TOOLS

"We have much to do together,

Let us do in wisdom and joy and love.

Let us make this the Human Experience."

Gary Zukav, *The Seal of the Soul*

After the extensive work you have done so far to understand and change the emotional, thinking and behavioral manifestations of your insecure attachment style, I know it may be difficult to remember all of it or to know where to start. In this section I am presenting some useful "cheat sheets" that you can review any time you need to while you continue your work.

First, I have put together the following summary of the emotions, thoughts and behaviors that we have covered so far. You can quickly review them when things get difficult and can aspire to break the typical negative cycle in order to bring you closer to a secure style. Keep it handy, and I hope it helps you!

Anxious Individuals can:

Answer the following questions before calling for a fight:

- What is the specific issue I want to address?
- How exactly am I feeling about it? Try to clear the ball of emotions.
- Am I able to express my feelings regardless of the fear of conflict or upsetting my partner?
- Am I able and ready to express my feelings/anger in a constructive healthy way?
- Am I capable of listening as much as talking?
- Am I capable of controlling myself and not overreacting in the moment when I hear something I disagree with or that I interpret as hurtful?
- Am I willing to use "I" statements to express my feelings instead of making generalized right or wrong statements, criticizing or finger pointing?
- Am I able to propose some specific solutions, ask for specific requests that are realistic and keep in mind both of our needs?

Additional tools:

- Keep close friends, attend therapy, and create a network of

people that understand and support your emotions.
- Take care of yourself. Engage in soothing and relaxing activities. Do not wait for your partner or others to take care of you. You will set yourself up for disappointment.
- Learn to identify and express your needs. Don't expect people to read your mind.

Avoidant Individuals can:

Answer the following questions before running away physically or emotionally:

- How exactly am I feeling about it? Try to stay connected to your deepest feelings. Do not be afraid of being vulnerable.
- Am I able to express my feelings as best as I can and acknowledge my partner's without ridiculing or disregarding them?
- Am I able to stay focused in how my partner's demands and feelings make me feel?
- Am I capable of listening instead of becoming defensive?
- Am I capable of staying present and engaged when I hear something I disagree with or that I interpret as hurtful?
- Am I willing to use validating statements instead of providing solutions or justifications, and just stay in the moment?
- Am I able to propose a time to reconnect and take the initiative to do so when I say I will?
- Am I willing to hear my partner's solutions and ask for specific

requests that are realistic and keep in mind both of our needs?

Additional tools:

- Take an active role in initiating and promoting connectedness with your partner and deepen other intimate relationships (parents, friends, attending therapy...)
- Continue to try to see conflict as a positive ingredient for change and improvement of the relationship
- Announce when you need space and determine a specific period of time. Reconnect with love and warmth even when you don't feel like it.

Secondly, I would like to offer a summary of the common traits anxious and avoidant styles present as well as what they need to work on to continue to move towards a secure attachment style. Keep this list handy to track your progress:

Pursuer Common Traits	Pursuer Growth Options	Distancer Common Traits	Distancer Growth Option
Initiates	Learn to wait	Reacts	Initiate
Desires and pursues closeness	Expand life outside of relationship,	Desires and craves personal space	Decreases other distractions

Relationally-oriented	develops fuller individual aspect of self		Self-oriented	and look for closeness towards partner
	Take breaks from relationship			Becomes more interested in other person's life and responding to other's feelings and needs
Wants stability in relationship			Wants adventure	
	Learn to accept that disconnection and mistakes will happen (shouldn't be the pattern)			Looks for excitement opportunities within relationship
Uses more words in general. Uses more feelings words			Uses fewer words in general. Uses more facts words	Balance work with relationships

	Make direct requests		Initiates conversation about the relationship and becomes more attuned and talkative about feelings and details
Criticizes and attacks: more aggressiveness		Defends and minimizes: more passive-aggressiveness	
Usually more pessimistic. Over focuses on problems. This could be a positive and negative trait.	Control emotions and reduce anger. Tries to focus also on facts.	Usually more positive. Not aware of problems. This could be a positive and negative trait.	Looks into what partner presents with open mind to see valid points and looks into sublet behavior that triggers others
	Acknowledge positive things about self, partner,		Acknowledge negative feelings and things about

Doubts self. Needs reassurance	relationship and/or world	Protect self. Needs to be proved right	self, relationship and world
Feels: deprived	Learns to see value in her way of being and ask for validation when pertinent. Does not believe it is just his/her fault, being called crazy or over dramatic.	Feels: overwhelmed, coerced Deepest fear: being controlled, losing self	Welcome criticism and improving suggestions without taking them as a personal attack.
Deepest fear: abandonment, feeling crazy			Maintain emotional balance and

Love=time together, words of appreciation, touch Views negativity as a motivation for change	Maintain emotional balance when receiving a "no." Try to not maximize See differences as part of life and not as a threat. Accept imperfection, separation and differentiation	Love=acts of service, gifts, words of affirmation Views negativity as something threatening and a sign to quit Extra thoughts:	stay connected in the presence of negativity. Try to not minimize. See being influenced by partners and closeness as opportunities for growth and union vs. threat Accepts and try to give other gestures of love.

Extra thoughts:	Accepts and tries to take in other gestures of love. Communicate positive and negative words at the same time with less intensity. Maintain focus on conversation topic and		Stay with negative information while maintaining self-esteem and increase self-efficacy vs giving up Expand emotional life and see pain and emotions as part of life and not as a waste of time or something detrimental.

	include factual information		Remember what is promised and deliver
	Reduce complaints		Be more affectionate /romantic
	Be seductive without manipulation		

And finally, the following chart presents another summary of the complex dimensions of insecure attachment and how to repair it:

Attachment Styles Characteristics & Repairing Steps Chart

	Avoidant	**Anxious**
Self-Talk	"I can't get close to you because you will smother me and complicate my life." "I am afraid to depend on you and afraid to want to"	"You don't love me unless you validate and meet all my needs." "I can't depend on you"
Scripted Behavior	Distancing, disconnection, passive – aggressive. Avoidance of intimacy and commitment Ambivalence and withholding	Craves intimacy and commitment. Reactive "distancing" Insisting and conflictive
Response to Conflict	Disconnects and distances Blames and punishes Physical discomfort Invalidates Wants peace at any price Avoids reconnection	Demands, blames, and chastises as a way to get movement. Invalidates Wants resolution at any price

			Feels anxiety and pushes for reconnection too soon
To Rewrite the script		Learn to connect, disconnect, and reconnect more smoothly and by announcing and preparing partner for your movements. Move forward (closer) when you want to distance. Express your needs and fears Share your wounds. Validate your partner's needs even if you don't agree with them. Try to not get hurt by the other person's words or upsets. Try to risk and confront,	Learn to get comfortable with movements between connection, disconnecting, and reconnection. Announce your need for connection. Move back, when you want to pursue. Express your needs and fears. Share your wounds. Validate your partner's feelings even if you don't agree with them or get hurt by them. Desensitize yourself to rejection and

	even if the other person is upset.	abandonment to ease your anxiety.

Reprinted from Make Up, Don't Break Up 2nd edition by Dr. Bonnie Eaker Weil. Copyright (c) 2010, 2000, 1999 by Dr. Bonnie Eaker Weil. Used by permission of Adams Media, an F+W Media, Inc Co. All rights reserved.

The most important thing I would like to leave you with is this: be encouraged and persevere! Thanks to the advances in science and the discovery of neuroplasticity we know for a fact that a secure attachment style *can* be achieved. As with anything worthy in life, it requires work, time, and dedication. Many factors can contribute to our overall well-being: temperament, personality types, and circumstances. But attachment can be the most influential factor when it comes to relationships and one of the most important ones when it comes to overall health and life coping. Because we are just beginning to understand this, people often still detour, investing immense amount of time and money in good nutrition, exercise, pills, and exotic practices etc, which are ok, but might continue to take care of one aspect alone instead of the overall picture. Fortunately for us, in the last decade there have been many passionate and dedicated people studying the science of love and relationships and therefore, there is more information about our topic.

I remember in one of my first relationships workshops, Ellen Purcell, from the PAIRS Relationships Mastery program said,

"Nowadays we do all this work and study because for people to stay together is a choice and not an obligation anymore." I find that to be so true. People don't want to resign themselves to live in unhealthy and unhappy relationships, as many of our grandparents and parents had to do. But in order to achieve a positive outcome we need to make a conscious decision to break the chain. Otherwise, because of the trauma reenactment process, we may simply repeat the negative patterns and decisions over and over even when we don't want to. It is my wish that the information and tools in this book provide you with some light, hope and empowerment in your journey. It is not easy, but it is one of the most human and rewarding experiences you will ever have!

So remember: go counter-intuitive of what you tend to do in order to reverse the pattern of your original attachment style. See yourself and your partner as a wounded child. Only with compassion for you and others can we overcome the difficult times. With positive new life experiences, appropriate therapeutic intervention when necessary, and a strong desire for change, we can alter our relationships and experience true intimacy and closeness.

"We are never so vulnerable as when we love."

Freud

"We know that love makes us vulnerable, but we also know that we are never as safe as strong as when we are sure we are loved."

Sue Johnson, Ph.D.

"Romantic love glues us together, yet real love is born in relationship. While our conscious mind wants us to feel happy all the time, our unconscious mind has another agenda- and that is, to grow up, finish childhood, and become conscious that we have been reacting to painful experiences with the same unconscious patterns that we inherited from our childhood."

Harville Hendrix, PhD.

"Perfect love is rare indeed, for to be a lover will require that you continually have the subtlety of the very wise, the flexibility of the child, the sensitivity of the artist, the understanding of the philosopher, the acceptance of the saint, the tolerance of the scholar and the fortitude of the certain."

Leo Buscaglia

"Central to the science of attachment is the discovery that our need to be in a close relationship is embedded in our genes; so, contrary to what many relationship experts today may tell us about the importance of remaining emotionally 'self-sufficient,' attachment research shows us that our need to be close to our partner is essential. That, in fact, we can't live without it."

Levine & Heller, Attached, 2010

Recommendations for Finding a Therapist

"Three human experiences have been documented as promoting well-being: secure attachment, mindfulness meditation, and effective psychotherapy. You will explore how these systems share similar neural mechanisms and the implications that this has for both attaining a state of well-being and transforming the brain." (Siegel, 2012) So if you are really determined to change your life, investing in therapy would be the way to go. Yes, I am biased of course, but hopefully it is clear by now that we are relational beings. Therefore, you will get the most results when working on your relationship issues within the context of a relationship!

Attachment is our ability to form emotional bonds and empathic, enjoyable relationships with other people, especially close family members. Attachment issues are most obvious and prevalent during childhood, and are often the result of abuse or neglect. The inability to form healthy, secure attachments is sure to cause disruptions to people socially and emotionally. Attachment is related to trust, empathy, and self-esteem. As you can imagine by now the importance is huge and the investment quiet significant. So you want to look carefully. Spending some time in looking for the right match is the first step.

So here some suggestions about what to look for in a therapist:

1. First and most important you need to feel comfortable and trust the person. That is a common rule for any type of therapy.

2. The therapist has to have training and experience in relationships with a perspective on attachment and early childhood focus. Some modalities to look for are: Emotionally Focus Therapy or EFT, Imago therapists, Internal Family Systems or IFS and Ego States Psychotherapies.

An Attachment Therapist is a necessary ingredient for an effective healing process. However, the specialty isn't very common so don't hesitate to ask directly if in his/her practice he/she uses an attachment based approach. Some people that advertise themselves as relationships experts use the approach. Why this theory? Because attachment does something that is rare in psychology: it combines the pleasures of testable hypotheses with the prospect of changing the world.

"I really do think that this work has great relevance to the well-being and happiness of mankind," Ainsworth says. "It sounds corny, and I don't go around shouting it from the rooftops, but that's what's behind the whole thing as far as I'm concerned."

REFERENCES AND RECOMMENDED READINGS:

Bartholomew, K. & Horowitz, L. M. (1991). Attachment Styles Among Young Adults: A Test of a Four-Category Model. *Journal of Personality and Social Psychology*, 61(2), 226-244

Baumeister, R.F. & Leary, M.R. (1995). The Need to Belong: Desire for Interpersonal Attachments as a Fundamental Human Motivation. *Psychological Bulletin,* 117, 497-529

Becker-Phelps, L. (2014). *Insecure In Love: How Anxious Attachment Can Make You Feel Jealous, Needy, and Worried and What You Can Do About It.* Oakland, CA: New Harbinger.

Berzoff, J., Melano L, & Hertz, P. (2011*). Inside Out and Outside In: Psychodynamic Clinical Theory and Psychopathology.* Plymouth, PY: Rowman and Littlefield Publishers, Inc.

Bretherton, I. (1990). The Origins of Attachment: John Bolwby and Mary Ainsworth. *Developmental Psychology*, 28, 759-775.

Cassidy, J., and Mohr, J. J. (2001). Unsolvable Fear, Trauma, and Psychopathology: Theory, Research, and Clinical Considerations Related to Disorganized Attachment Across the Life Span. *Clinical Psychology: Science and Practice*, 8, 275–298.

Cassidy, J. & Shaver, P. R. (2008). Handbook of Attachment: Theory, Research, and Clinical Applications. *New York, NY: The Guildford Press.*

Chapman, G. D. (2015). The 5 Love Languages: The Secret to Love that Lasts. *Chicago, IL: Northfield Publishing.*

Diamond, S. (2008). *Essential Secrets of Psychotherapy: The Inner Child.* Psychology Today. *[Online].* Retrieved from https://www.psychologytoday.com/blog/evil-deeds/200806/essential-secrets-psychotherapy-the-inner-child

Diener, E. & Biswas-Diener, R. (2008). *Happiness: Unlocking the Mysteries of Psychological Wealth.* Oxford, UK: Blackwell

Eaker, B. W. (2010). *Make Up, Don't Break Up.* Avon, MA: Adams Media.

Evergreen Consultants in Human Behavior (2013). *Adult attachment disorder and treatment.* [Online]. Retrieved from http://www.attachmenttherapy.com/adult.htm

Feil, N. (2012). *The Validation Breakthrough.* Baltimore, MD: Health Professions Press.

Feeny, B. C. (2007). The Dependency Paradox in Close Relationships: Accepting Dependence Promotes Independence. *Journal of Personality and Social Psychology,* 92(2), 268-285

Firestone, L. F. (2013). What is Your Attachment Style? *Psychalive* [Online]. Retrieve from http://www.psychalive.org/how-your-attachment-style-impacts-your-relationship/

Firestone, R. W, Firestone, L. F., Catlet, J. & Love, P. (2002). *Conquer Your Critical Inner Voice: A Revolutionary Program to Counter Negative Thoughts and Live Free from Imagined.* New York, NY: New Harbinger Publications.

Gordon, L. H. (1990). *Love Knots: How to Untangle Those Everyday Frustrations and Arguments that Keep You From Being With the One You Love.* PAIRS Foundation, Ltd: Dell.

Harley, W. F. (2001). *His Needs, Her Needs. Building an Affair-Proofed Marriage.* Grand Rapids, MI: Fleming H. Revell.

Hazan, C., & Shaver, P. R. (1987). Romantic Love Conceptualized as an Attachment Process. *Journal of Personality and Social Psychology,* 52, 511-524.

Hendrix, H. (1998). *Getting the Love You Want.* New York, NY: Holt Paperbacks.

Johnson, S. (2013). *Love Sense: the Revolutionary New Science of Romantic Relationships.* New York, NY: Little, Brown and Company.

Johnson, S. (2008). *Hold Me Tight: Seven Conversations for a Lifetime of Love.* New York, NY: Hachette Book Group.

Jones, S. M. (2005). Attachment Style Differences and Similarities in Evaluations of Affective Communication Skills and Person-centered

Comforting Messages. *Western Journal of Communication,* (69)3, 233–249.

Lefton, L. A. & Brannon, L. (2005). *Psychology.* Boston, MA: Allyn & Bacon.

McLeod, S. A. (2009). *Attachment Theory.* [Online]. Retrieved from http://www.simplypsychology.org/attachment.html

Levine, A., & Heller, R. (2010). *Attached: the New Science of Adult Attachment and How it Can Help You Find and Keep Love.* New York, NY: Penguin Book.

Lewis, T., Amini, F., & Lannon, R. (2001). *General Theory of Love.* New York, NY: Vintage Books.

Lucas, M. (2013). *Rewire Your Brain for Love: Creating Vibrant Relationships Using the Science of Mindfulness.* India: Hay House Publishers India.

Lumiere, MFT, L. M, (2012). *The Ultimate Secure Base: Healing Insecure Attachment in the Nondual Field.* [Online]. Retrieved from http://undividedjournal.com/2012/11/29/the-ultimate-secure-base-healing-insecure-attachment-in-the-nondual-field/

Maccoby, E. (1980) *Social Development: Psychological Growth and the Parent-child Relationship.* San Diego, CA: Harcourt Brace Jovanovich.

Maisel, N.C. & Gable, S.L. (2009) For Richer…in Good Times…and in Health: Positive Processes in Relationships. In S.J.

Lopez & C.R. Snyder (Eds.) *Oxford Handbook of Positive Psychology.* NY: Oxford University Press.

Margaret, P. & Chopich, E. (1990). Inner Bonding: Becoming a Loving Adult to You. New York, NY: HarperCollins.

Mellody, P., Wells Miller, A., & Miller, J. K. (2003). *Facing Love Addiction: Giving Yourself the Power to Change the Way You Love.* New York, NY: HarperCollins.

Mellody, B. (2009). *The New Codependency: Help and Guidance for Today's Generation.* New York, NY: Simon & Schuster.

Mikulincer, M. Florian, V., Tolmacz, R. (1990). Attachment Styles and Fear of Personal Death: A Case Study of Affect Regulation. *Journal of Personality and Social Psychology*, 58(2), 273-280.

Pietromonaco, P.R., Greenwood, D., & Barrett, L. F. (2004). Conflict in Adult Close Relationships: an Attachment Perspective. In W. S. Rholes & J. A. Simpson (Eds.), *Adult attachment: New directions and emerging issue (*pp. 267-299). New York: Guilford Press.

Pietromonaco, P.R., Greenwood, D., & Barrett, L. F. (1997). Working Models of Attachment and Daily Social Interactions. *Journal of Personality and Social Psychology,* 73(6), 1409-1423.

Pistole, M. C. (1989). Attachment in Adult Romantic Relationships: Style of Conflict Resolution and Relationship Satisfaction. *Journal of Social and Personal Relationships,* 6, 505-510.

Potter, D & Sullivan, K. *Attachment Difficulties, Childhood, Trauma and Reactive Attachment Disorder: Clinical Guidelines for Assessment, Diagnosis and Treatment.* Center for Child and Family Health and Duke University Medical Center.

Ryan, R.M. & Deci, E.D. (2001) On Happiness and Human Potentials: A Review of Research on Hedonic and Eudaimonic Well-Being. *Annual Review of Psychology,* 52, 141-66

Ryff, C. (1989). Happiness is Everything, or Is It? Explorations on the Meaning of Psychological Well-Being. *Journal of Personality and Social Psychology, 6, 1069-81.*

Shapiro, F. (2013). *Getting Past Your Past: Take Control of Your Life with Self-Help Techniques from EMDR Therapy.* New York, NY: Rodale Books.

Schwartz, R. C. (1997). *Internal Family Systems Therapy.* New York, NY: The Guilford Press.

Seligman, M.E.P. (2011). *Flourish: A Visionary New Understanding of Happiness and Well-Being.* New York: Free Press.

Shaver, R.P. & Mikulincer, M. (2012). An Attachment Perspective on Psychopathology. *World Psychiatry,* 11, 11-15.

Shaver, R.P. & Mikulincer, M. (2007). Adult Attachment Strategies and the Regulation of Emotion. In Gross, J. J. (Ed.), *Handbook of Emotion Regulation* (pp. 446-465). New York, NY: The Guildford Press.

Segal, J. & Jaffe, J. (2015) Attachment and Adult Relationships. *Harvard University.* [Online]. Retrieved from http://www.helpguide.org/articles/relationships/attachment-and-adult-relationships.htm

Schmidt, S. J (2009). The Developmental Needs Strategy Protocol. An Ego State Therapy for Healing Adults With Childhood Trauma and Attachment Wounds. San Antonio, TX: DNMS Institute.

Shi, L. (2003). *The Association Between Adult Attachment Styles and Conflict Resolution in Romantic Relationships.* American Journal of Family Therapy, 31(3), 143-157.

Siegel, D. J. (2012). *The Developing Mind: How Relationships and the Brain Interact to Share Who We Are.* New York, NY: The Guildford press.

Siegel, D. J. & Bryson, T. P. (2012). *The Whole-Brain Child: 12 Revolutionary Strategies to Nurture Your Child's Developing Mind.* New York, NY: Bantam Books.

Siegel, D. J. (2010). *Mindsight: the New Science of Personal Transformation.* New York, NY: Bantam Books.

Sroufe, L. A. (1997). *Emotional Development: The Organization of Emotional Life in the Early Years.* New York, NY: Cambridge University Press

Tatkin, S. (2012). *Wired for Love: How Understanding Your Partner's Brain and Attachment Style Can Help You Defuse Conflict and Build a Secure Relationship.* Okland, CA: New Harbinger Publications.

Weinhold, J. B. & Weinhold, B.K. (2008). *Counter-Dependency: the Flight from Intimacy.* Novato, CA: New World Library.

Made in the
USA
Lexington, KY